DOVER · THRIFT · EDITIONS

The Birds

ARISTOPHANES

DOVER PUBLICATIONS, INC.
Mineola, New York

DOVER THRIFT EDITIONS

GENERAL EDITOR: PAUL NEGRI
EDITOR OF THIS VOLUME: JOSLYN T. PINE

Copyright

Note copyright © 1999 by Dover Publications, Inc.
All rights reserved under Pan American and International Copyright Conventions.

Published in Canada by General Publishing Company, Ltd., 30 Lesmill Road, Don Mills, Toronto, Ontario.

Bibliographical Note

This Dover edition, first published in 1999, is an unabridged republication of the anonymous translation that originally appeared in *Aristophanes: the Eleven Comedies*, published by Horace Liveright, New York, 1928, on a subscription basis. All of the translator's footnotes are included. The introductory Note has been specially prepared for this edition.

Library of Congress Cataloging-in-Publication Data

Aristophanes.
    [Birds. English]
    The birds / Aristophanes.
        p.   cm. — (Dover thrift editions)
    ISBN 0-486-40886-8 (pbk.)
    1. Greek drama (Comedy)—Translations into English.   2. Athens (Greece)—
Social life and customs—Drama.   3. Birds—Drama.   I. Title.   II. Series.
PA3877.A8   1999
882'.01—dc21   99-25512
                                                                           CIP

Manufactured in the United States of America
Dover Publications, Inc., 31 East 2nd Street, Mineola, N.Y. 11501

Note

Aristophanes (c.446 B.C.–c.385 B.C.), poet, playwright, and comic genius, was the author of forty plays, only eleven of which are extant. Little is known about his life other than what has been inferred from his plays. He was probably born in Athens, Greece, the son of a wealthy man—Philippus—who owned property on the island of Aegina. As such, Aristophanes could identify himself as a member of the conservative class of society known as the "knights"—a rank somewhere between the wealthy aristocracy and the peasant underclass. He embraced the role of the artist in Athenian society, holding an allegorical mirror up to his times to parody the moral conflicts and intellectual turmoil of the period, particularly those inflicted by the Peloponnesian War—the struggle between Athens and Sparta that spanned 431 B.C.–404 B.C.

The origins of comedy may be traced to the Festivals of Dionysus in ancient Athens, the showcase for such plays as Aristophanes' *The Birds*. Here Priapus was worshipped side by side with Bacchus, and exuberant fertility rites carried the sanction of religion. In the same spirit of celebration, ribald and licentious material was part of the very texture of these performances, and not surprisingly, women and children were barred from entrance to these entertainments.

Aristophanes' plays (except *Plutus*, 388 B.C.) are the only surviving examples of the Athenian Old Comedy form, aside from fragments. Old Comedy is satirical in nature, festive in spirit, and notably modern in being free of many of the restraints on subject and style that bound the literary productions of Homer, Sophocles, and Thucydides— among many others. In fact, generally speaking, Aristophanic drama has more in common with burlesque, vaudeville, musical farce, comic opera, and pantomime than it has with earlier and more serious works of the ancient Greeks. In addition to their entertainment value, the plays functioned as social critiques for the Athenian public, standing in for the political caricature, the literary review, and the propagandist pamphlet of today.

The New Comedy, on the other hand, arose after Athens had fallen under Macedonian rule, and politics was completely excluded from the stage. Its chief practitioners were Philomen and Menander, and it was the ancestor of the comedy of manners that came to dominate European theatre for twenty-three centuries. The New Comedy was characterized by a universality of its elements—the problems and relationships of Everyman; unlike the Old Comedy, it wasn't heavily grounded in the particulars of the time and place of its creation. So it is clearly a tribute to Aristophanes' brilliant wit and lyric gifts that—despite their Old Comedy form—his plays have nonetheless transcended their apparently limited context and continue to be studied and performed to the present day.

Of Aristophanes' eleven surviving plays, *The Birds* (414 B.C.) is his acknowledged masterpiece. It was a parody of utopianism written a generation before Plato's *Republic*—the first literary utopian work. Some scholars view *The Birds* as purely a comedy of fancy, while others perceive beneath the comic veneer a political significance, intended to satirize the imperialistic ambitions of the city that would soon suffer disastrous defeat in the Sicilian expedition (415–413 B.C.), an undertaking championed by Alcibiades, the Athenian politician and general who harbored utopian dreams.

In brief, the plot of *The Birds* depicts the scheme of two old Athenians—Euelpides (Optimistic) and Pisthetærus (Persuasive)—who are fed up with their sycophantic and litigious countrymen, and leave Attica to set up a utopian commonwealth in midair with the help of the famous King of the Birds (Epops, sometimes called Tereus), and his subject birds. Called "Cloud-cuckoo-town"—and situated between heaven and earth—the new city is guarded by the birds who, according to the Chorus, are the offspring of Eros and Chaos, and being older than the Olympians, are worthier of worship than the gods whom the utopian founders seek to supplant. Although the new utopia is plagued by a succession of charlatans and busybodies who seek to interfere with the new government—a real estate agent who wants to parcel the air into lots, a soothsayer with made-to-order oracles, and even a retailer of government decrees—people clamor to gain citizenship to Cloud-cuckoo-town, and even the gods of Olympus relinquish their sovereignty to the new rulers.

Dramatis Personæ

EUELPIDES
PISTHETÆRUS
EPOPS (the Hoopoe)
TROCHILUS, Servant to Epops
PHŒNICOPTERUS
HERALDS
A PRIEST
A POET
A PROPHET
METON, a Geometrician
A COMMISSIONER
A DEALER IN DECREES
IRIS
A PARRICIDE
CINESIAS, a Dithyrambic Bard
AN INFORMER
PROMETHEUS
POSIDON
TRIBALLUS
HERACLES
SERVANT OF PISTHETÆRUS
MESSENGERS
CHORUS OF BIRDS

SCENE: A wild, desolate tract of open country; broken rocks and brushwood occupy the centre of the stage.

The Birds

The Birds

EUELPIDES [*to his jay*][1]   Do you think I should walk straight for yon
tree?

PISTHETÆRUS [*to his crow*]   Cursed beast, what are you croaking to
me? . . . to retrace my steps?

EUELPIDES   Why, you wretch, we are wandering at random, we are
exerting ourselves only to return to the same spot; 'tis labour lost.

PISTHETÆRUS   To think that I should trust to this crow, which has
made me cover more than a thousand furlongs!

EUELPIDES   And I to this jay, who has torn every nail from my fingers!

PISTHETÆRUS   If only I knew where we were. . . .

EUELPIDES   Could you find your country again from here?

PISTHETÆRUS   No, I feel quite sure I could not, any more than could
Execestides[2] find his.

EUELPIDES   Oh dear! oh dear!

PISTHETÆRUS   Aye, aye, my friend, 'tis indeed the road of "oh dears"
we are following.

EUELPIDES   That Philocrates, the bird-seller, played us a scurvy trick,
when he pretended these two guides could help us to find Tereus,[3]

[1]Euelpides is holding a jay and Pisthetærus a crow; they are the guides who are to lead
them to the kingdom of the birds.

[2]A stranger who wanted to pass as an Athenian, although coming originally from a far-
away barbarian country.

[3]A king of Thrace, a son of Ares, who married Procné, the daughter of Pandion, King
of Athens, whom he had assisted against the Megarians. He violated his sister-in-law,
Philomela, and then cut out her tongue; she nevertheless managed to convey to her
sister how she had been treated. They both agreed to kill Itys, whom Procné had borne
to Tereus, and dished up the limbs of his own son to the father; at the end of the meal
Philomela appeared and threw the child's head upon the table. Tereus rushed with
drawn sword upon the princesses, but all the actors in this terrible scene were meta-
morphised. Tereus became an Epops (hoopoe), Procné a swallow, Philomela a
nightingale, and Itys a goldfinch. According to Anacreon and Apollodorus it was
Procné who became the nightingale and Philomela the swallow, and this is the version
of the tradition followed by Aristophanes.

1

the Epops, who is a bird, without being born of one. He has indeed sold us this jay, a true son of Tharelides,[1] for an obolus, and this crow for three, but what can they do? Why, nothing whatever but bite and scratch!—What's the matter with you then, that you keep opening your beak? Do you want us to fling ourselves headlong down these rocks? There is no road that way.

PISTHETÆRUS   Not even the vestige of a track in any direction.

EUELPIDES   And what does the crow say about the road to follow?

PISTHETÆRUS   By Zeus, it no longer croaks the same thing it did.

EUELPIDES   And which way does it tell us to go now?

PISTHETÆRUS   It says that, by dint of gnawing, it will devour my fingers.

EUELPIDES   What misfortune is ours! we strain every nerve to get to the birds,[2] do everything we can to that end, and we cannot find our way! Yes, spectators, our madness is quite different from that of Sacas. He is not a citizen, and would fain be one at any cost; we, on the contrary, born of an honourable tribe and family and living in the midst of our fellow-citizens, we have fled from our country as hard as ever we could go. 'Tis not that we hate it; we recognize it to be great and rich, likewise that everyone has the right to ruin himself; but the crickets only chirrup among the fig-trees for a month or two, whereas the Athenians spend their whole lives in chanting forth judgments from their law-courts.[3] That is why we started off with a basket, a stewpot and some myrtle boughs[4] and have come to seek a quiet country in which to settle. We are going to Tereus, the Epops, to learn from him, whether, in his aerial flights, he has noticed some town of this kind.

PISTHETÆRUS   Here! look!

EUELPIDES   What's the matter?

PISTHETÆRUS   Why, the crow has been pointing me to something up there for some time now.

EUELPIDES   And the jay is also opening its beak and craning its neck to show me I know not what. Clearly, there are some birds about here. We shall soon know, if we kick up a noise to start them.

PISTHETÆRUS   Do you know what to do? Knock your leg against this rock.

EUELPIDES   And you your head to double the noise.

---

[1]An Athenian who had some resemblance to a jay.
[2]Literally, *to go to the crows*, a proverbial expression equivalent to our *going to the devil*.
[3]They leave Athens because of their hatred of lawsuits and informers; this is the especial failing of the Athenians satirized in 'The Wasps.'
[4]Myrtle boughs were used in sacrifices, and the founding of every colony was started by a sacrifice.

PISTHETÆRUS   Well then use a stone instead; take one and hammer with it.

EUELPIDES   Good idea! Ho there, within! Slave! slave!

PISTHETÆRUS   What's that, friend! You say, "slave," to summon Epops! 'Twould be much better to shout, "Epops, Epops!"

EUELPIDES   Well then, Epops! Must I knock again? Epops!

TROCHILUS   Who's there? Who calls my master?

EUELPIDES   Apollo the Deliverer! what an enormous beak![1]

TROCHILUS   Good god! they are bird-catchers.

EUELPIDES   The mere sight of him petrifies me with terror. What a horrible monster!

TROCHILUS   Woe to you!

EUELPIDES   But we are not men.

TROCHILUS   What are you, then?

EUELPIDES   I am the Fearling, an African bird.

TROCHILUS   You talk nonsense.

EUELPIDES   Well, then, just ask it of my feet.[2]

TROCHILUS   And this other one, what bird is it?

PISTHETÆRUS   I? I am a Cackling,[3] from the land of the pheasants.

EUELPIDES   But you yourself, in the name of the gods! what animal are you?

TROCHILUS   Why, I am a slave-bird.

EUELPIDES   Why, have you been conquered by a cock?

TROCHILUS   No, but when my master was turned into a peewit, he begged me to become a bird too, to follow and to serve him.

EUELPIDES   Does a bird need a servant, then?

TROCHILUS   'Tis no doubt because he was a man. At times he wants to eat a dish of loach from Phalerum; I seize my dish and fly to fetch him some. Again he wants some pea-soup; I seize a ladle and a pot and run to get it.

EUELPIDES   This is, then, truly a running-bird.[4] Come, Trochilus, do us the kindness to call your master.

TROCHILUS   Why, he has just fallen asleep after a feed of myrtle-berries and a few grubs.

EUELPIDES   Never mind; wake him up.

TROCHILUS   I am certain he will be angry. However, I will wake him to please you.

PISTHETÆRUS   You cursed brute! why, I am almost dead with terror!

[1]The actors wore masks made to resemble the birds they were supposed to represent.
[2]Fear had had disastrous effects upon Euelpides' internal economy, and this his feet evidenced.
[3]The same mishap had occurred to Pisthetærus.
[4]The Greek word for *wren* is derived from the same root as the Greek verb *to run*.

EUELPIDES   Oh! my god! 'twas sheer fear that made me lose my jay.

PISTHETÆRUS   Ah! you great coward! were you so frightened that you let go your jay?

EUELPIDES   And did you not lose your crow, when you fell sprawling on the ground? Pray tell me that.

PISTHETÆRUS   No, no.

EUELPIDES   Where is it, then?

PISTHETÆRUS   It has flown away.

EUELPIDES   Then you did not let it go! Oh! you brave fellow!

EPOPS   Open the forest,[1] that I may go out!

EUELPIDES   By Heracles! what a creature! what plumage! What means this triple crest?

EPOPS   Who wants me?

EUELPIDES   The twelve great gods have used you ill, meseems.

EPOPS   Are you chaffing me about my feathers? I have been a man, strangers.

EUELPIDES   'Tis not you we are jeering at.

EPOPS   At what, then?

EUELPIDES   Why, 'tis your beak that looks so odd to us.

EPOPS   This is how Sophocles outrages me in his tragedies. Know, I once was Tereus.[2]

EUELPIDES   You were Tereus, and what are you now? a bird or a peacock?[3]

EPOPS   I am a bird.

EUELPIDES   Then where are your feathers? For I don't see them.

EPOPS   They have fallen off.

EUELPIDES   Through illness?

EPOPS   No. All birds moult their feathers, you know, every winter, and others grow in their place. But tell me, who are you?

EUELPIDES   We? We are mortals.

EPOPS   From what country?

EUELPIDES   From the land of the beautiful galleys.[4]

EPOPS   Are you dicasts?[5]

---

[1]No doubt there was some scenery to represent a forest. Besides, there is a pun intended. In Greek, the words answering for *forests* and *doors* only differ slightly in sound.

[2]Sophocles had written a tragedy about Tereus, in which, no doubt, the king finally appears as a hoopoe.

[3]One would expect the question to be "*bird or man.*"—Are you a peacock? The hoopoe resembles the peacock inasmuch as both have crests.

[4]Athens.

[5]The Athenians were madly addicted to lawsuits.

EUELPIDES   No, if anything, we are anti-dicasts.

EPOPS   Is that kind of seed sown among you?[1]

EUELPIDES   You have to look hard to find even a little in our fields.

EPOPS   What brings you here?

EUELPIDES   We wish to pay you a visit.

EPOPS   What for?

EUELPIDES   Because you formerly were a man, like we are, formerly you had debts, as we have, formerly you did not want to pay them, like ourselves; furthermore, being turned into a bird, you have when flying seen all lands and seas. Thus you have all human knowledge as well as that of birds. And hence we have come to you to beg you to direct us to some cosy town, in which one can repose as if on thick coverlets.

EPOPS   And are you looking for a greater city than Athens?

EUELPIDES   No, not a greater, but one more pleasant to dwell in.

EPOPS   Then you are looking for an aristocratic country.

EUELPIDES   I? Not at all! I hold the son of Scellias in horror.[2]

EPOPS   But, after all, what sort of city would please you best?

EUELPIDES   A place where the following would be the most important business transacted. — Some friend would come knocking at the door quite early in the morning saying, "By Olympian Zeus, be at my house early, as soon as you have bathed, and bring your children too. I am giving a nuptial feast, so don't fail, or else don't cross my threshold when I am in distress."

EPOPS   Ah! that's what may be called being fond of hardships. And what say you?

PISTHETÆRUS   My tastes are similar.

EPOPS   And they are?

PISTHETÆRUS   I want a town where the father of a handsome lad will stop in the street and say to me reproachfully as if I had failed him, "Ah! Is this well done, Stilbonides! You met my son coming from the bath after the gymnasium and you neither spoke to him, nor embraced him, nor took him with you, nor ever once twitched his parts. Would anyone call you an old friend of mine?"

EPOPS   Ah! wag, I see you are fond of suffering. But there is a city of delights, such as you want. 'Tis on the Red Sea.

---

[1] As much as to say, *Then you have such things as anti-dicasts?* And Euelpides practically replies, *Very few.*

[2] His name was Aristocrates; he was a general and commanded a fleet sent in aid of Corcyra.

EUELPIDES   Oh, no. Not a sea-port, where some fine morning the Salaminian[1] galley can appear, bringing a writ-server along. Have you no Greek town you can propose to us?

EPOPS   Why not choose Lepreum in Elis for your settlement?

EUELPIDES   By Zeus! I could not look at Lepreum without disgust, because of Melanthius.[2]

EPOPS   Then, again, there is the Opuntian, where you could live.

EUELPIDES   I would not be Opuntian[3] for a talent. But come, what is it like to live with the birds? You should know pretty well.

EPOPS   Why, 'tis not a disagreeable life. In the first place, one has no purse.

EUELPIDES   That does away with much roguery.

EPOPS   For food the gardens yield us white sesamé, myrtle-berries, poppies and mint.

EUELPIDES   Why, 'tis the life of the newly-wed indeed.[4]

PISTHETÆRUS   Ha! I am beginning to see a great plan, which will transfer the supreme power to the birds, if you will but take my advice.

EPOPS   Take your advice? In what way?

PISTHETÆRUS   In what way? Well, firstly, do not fly in all directions with open beak; it is not dignified. Among us, when we see a thoughtless man, we ask, "What sort of bird is this?" and Teleas answers, "'Tis a man who has no brain, a bird that has lost his head, a creature you cannot catch, for it never remains in any one place."

EPOPS   By Zeus himself! your jest hits the mark. What then is to be done?

PISTHETÆRUS   Found a city.

EPOPS   We birds? But what sort of city should we build?

PISTHETÆRUS   Oh, really, really! 'tis spoken like a fool! Look down.

EPOPS   I am looking.

PISTHETÆRUS   Now look upwards.

EPOPS   I am looking.

PISTHETÆRUS   Turn your head round.

EPOPS   Ah! 'twill be pleasant for me, if I end in twisting my neck!

PISTHETÆRUS   What have you seen?

EPOPS   The clouds and the sky.

---

[1] The State galley, which carried the officials of the Athenian republic to their several departments and brought back those whose time had expired; it was this galley that was sent to Sicily to fetch back Alcibiades, who was accused of sacrilege.

[2] A tragic poet, who was a leper; there is a play, of course, on the word Lepreum.

[3] An allusion to Opuntius, who was one-eyed.

[4] The newly-married ate a sesamé-cake, decorated with garlands of myrtle, poppies, and mint.

PISTHETÆRUS   Very well! is not this the pole of the birds then?

EPOPS   How their pole?

PISTHETÆRUS   Or, if you like it, the land. And since it turns and passes through the whole universe, it is called, 'pole.'[1] If you build and fortify it, you will turn your pole into a fortified city.[2] In this way you will reign over mankind as you do over the grasshoppers and cause the gods to die of rabid hunger.

EPOPS   How so?

PISTHETÆRUS   The air is 'twixt earth and heaven. When we want to go to Delphi, we ask the Bœotians[3] for leave of passage; in the same way, when men sacrifice to the gods, unless the latter pay you tribute, you exercise the right of every nation towards strangers and don't allow the smoke of the sacrifices to pass through your city and territory.

EPOPS   By earth! by snares! by network![4] I never heard of anything more cleverly conceived; and, if the other birds approve, I am going to build the city along with you.

PISTHETÆRUS   Who will explain the matter to them?

EPOPS   You must yourself. Before I came they were quite ignorant, but since I have lived with them I have taught them to speak.

PISTHETÆRUS   But how can they be gathered together?

EPOPS   Easily. I will hasten down to the coppice to waken my dear Procné![5] as soon as they hear our voices, they will come to us hot wing.

PISTHETÆRUS   My dear bird, lose no time, I beg. Fly at once into the coppice and awaken Procné.

EPOPS   Chase off drowsy sleep, dear companion. Let the sacred hymn gush from thy divine throat in melodious strains; roll forth in soft cadence your refreshing melodies to bewail the fate of Itys,[6] which has been the cause of so many tears to us both. Your pure notes rise through the thick leaves of the yew-tree right up to the throne of Zeus, where Phœbus listens to you, Phœbus with his golden hair. And his ivory lyre responds to your plaintive accents; he gathers the choir of the gods and from their immortal lips rushes a sacred chant of blessed voices.   [*The flute is played behind the scene.*]

---

[1]From the Greek verb that means *to turn*.
[2]The Greek words for *pole* and *city* only differ by a single letter.
[3]Bœotia separated Attica from Phocis.
[4]He swears by the powers that are to him dreadful.
[5]As already stated, according to the legend accepted by Aristophanes, it was Procné who was turned into the nightingale.
[6]The son of Tereus and Procné.

PISTHETÆRUS   Oh! by Zeus! what a throat that little bird possesses. He has filled the whole coppice with honey-sweet melody!

EUELPIDES   Hush!

PISTHETÆRUS   What's the matter?

EUELPIDES   Will you keep silence?

PISTHETÆRUS   What for?

EUELPIDES   Epops is going to sing again.

EPOPS [*in the coppice*]   Epopoi, poi, popoi, epopoi, popoi, here, here, quick, quick, quick, my comrades in the air; all you, who pillage the fertile lands of the husbandmen, the numberless tribes who gather and devour the barley seeds, the swift flying race who sing so sweetly. And you whose gentle twitter resounds through the fields with the little cry of tio, tio, tio, tio, tio, tio, tio, tio; and you who hop about the branches of the ivy in the gardens; the mountain birds, who feed on the wild olive berries or the arbutus, hurry to come at my call, trioto, trioto, totobrix; you also, who snap up the sharp-stinging gnats in the marshy vales, and you who dwell in the fine plain of Marathon, all damp with dew, and you, the francolin with speckled wings; you too, the halcyons, who flit over the swelling waves of the sea, come hither to hear the tidings; let all the tribes of long-necked birds assemble here; know that a clever old man has come to us, bringing an entirely new idea and proposing great reforms. Let all come to the debate here, here, here, here. Torotorotorotorotix, kikkobau, kikkobau, torotorotorotorolililix.

PISTHETÆRUS   Can you see any bird?

EUELPIDES   By Phœbus, no! and yet I am straining my eyesight to scan the sky.

PISTHETÆRUS   'Twas really not worth Epops' while to go and bury himself in the thicket like a plover when a-hatching.

PHŒNICOPTERUS   Torotina, torotina.

PISTHETÆRUS   Hold, friend, here is another bird.

EUELPIDES   I' faith, yes! 'tis a bird, but of what kind? Isn't it a peacock?

PISTHETÆRUS   Epops will tell us. What is this bird?

EPOPS   'Tis not one of those you are used to seeing; 'tis a bird from the marshes.

PISTHETÆRUS   Oh! oh! but he is very handsome with his wings as crimson as flame.

EPOPS   Undoubtedly; indeed he is called flamingo.[1]

---

[1] An African bird, that comes to the southern countries of Europe, to Greece, Italy, and Spain; it is even seen in Provence.

EUELPIDES   Hi! I say! You!

PISTHETÆRUS   What are you shouting for?

EUELPIDES   Why, here's another bird.

PISTHETÆRUS   Aye, indeed; 'tis a foreign bird too. What is this bird from beyond the mountains with a look as solemn as it is stupid?

EPOPS   He is called the Mede.[1]

PISTHETÆRUS   The Mede! But, by Heracles! how, if a Mede, has he flown here without a camel?

EUELPIDES   Here's another bird with a crest.

PISTHETÆRUS   Ah! that's curious. I say, Epops, you are not the only one of your kind then?

EPOPS   This bird is the son of Philocles, who is the son of Epops;[2] so that, you see, I am his grandfather; just as one might say, Hipponicus,[3] the son of Callias, who is the son of Hipponicus.

PISTHETÆRUS   Then this bird is Callias! Why, what a lot of his feathers he has lost![4]

EPOPS   That's because he is honest; so the informers set upon him and the women too pluck out his feathers.

PISTHETÆRUS   By Posidon, do you see that many-coloured bird? What is his name?

EPOPS   This one? 'Tis the glutton.

PISTHETÆRUS   Is there another glutton besides Cleonymus? But why, if he is Cleonymus, has he not thrown away his crest?[5] But what is the meaning of all these crests? Have these birds come to contend for the double stadium prize?[6]

EPOPS   They are like the Carians, who cling to the crests of their mountains for greater safety.[7]

PISTHETÆRUS   Oh, Posidon! do you see what swarms of birds are gathering here?

---

[1]Aristophanes amusingly mixes up real birds with people and individuals, whom he represents in the form of birds; he is personifying the Medians here.

[2]Philocles, a tragic poet, had written a tragedy on Tereus, which was simply a plagiarism of the play of the same name by Sophocles. Philocles is the son of Epops, because he got his inspiration from Sophocles' Tereus, and at the same time is father to Epops, since he himself produced another Tereus.

[3]This Hipponicus is probably the orator whose ears Alcibiades boxed to gain a bet; he was a descendant of Callias, who was famous for his hatred of Pisistratus.

[4]This Callias, who must not be confounded with the foe of Pisistratus, had ruined himself.

[5]Cleonymus had cast away his shield; he was as great a glutton as he was a coward.

[6]A race in which the track had to be circled twice.

[7]A people of Asia Minor; when pursued by the Ionians they took refuge in the mountains.

EUELPIDES   By Phœbus! what a cloud! The entrance to the stage is no longer visible, so closely do they fly together.

PISTHETÆRUS   Here is the partridge.

EUELPIDES   Faith! there is the francolin.

PISTHETÆRUS   There is the poachard.

EUELPIDES   Here is the kingfisher. And over yonder?

EPOPS   'Tis the barber.

EUELPIDES   What? a bird a barber?

PISTHETÆRUS   Why, Sporgilus is one.[1] Here comes the owl.

EUELPIDES   And who is it brings an owl to Athens?[2]

PISTHETÆRUS   Here is the magpie, the turtle-dove, the swallow, the horned owl, the buzzard, the pigeon, the falcon, the ring-dove, the cuckoo, the red-foot, the red-cap, the purple-cap, the kestrel, the diver, the ousel, the osprey, the woodpecker.

EUELPIDES   Oh! oh! what a lot of birds! what a quantity of blackbirds! how they scold, how they come rushing up! What a noise! what a noise! Can they be bearing us ill-will? Oh! there! there! they are opening their beaks and staring at us.

PISTHETÆRUS   Why, so they are.

CHORUS   Popopopopopopopoi. Where is he who called me? Where am I to find him?

EPOPS   I have been waiting for you this long while! I never fail in my word to my friends.

CHORUS   Titititititititi. What good thing have you to tell me?

EPOPS   Something that concerns our common safety, and that is just as pleasant as it is to the purpose. Two men, who are subtle reasoners, have come here to seek me.

CHORUS   Where? What? What are you saying?

EPOPS   I say, two old men have come from the abode of men to propose a vast and splendid scheme to us.

CHORUS   Oh! 'tis a horrible, unheard-of crime! What are you saying?

EPOPS   Nay! never let my words scare you.

CHORUS   What have you done then?

EPOPS   I have welcomed two men, who wish to live with us.

CHORUS   And you have dared to do that!

EPOPS   Aye, and am delighted at having done so.

CHORUS   Where are they?

EPOPS   In your midst, as I am.

CHORUS   Ah! ah! we are betrayed; 'tis sacrilege! Our friend, he who

---

[1]An Athenian barber.

[2]The owl was dedicated to Athené, and being respected at Athens, it had greatly multiplied. Hence the proverb, *taking owl to Athens*, similar to our English *taking coals to Newcastle*.

picked up corn-seeds in the same plains as ourselves, has violated our ancient laws; he has broken the oaths that bind all birds; he has laid a snare for me, he has handed us over to the attacks of that impious race which, throughout all time, has never ceased to war against us. As for this traitorous bird, we will decide his case later, but the two old men shall be punished forthwith; we are going to tear them to pieces.

PISTHETÆRUS   'Tis all over with us.

EUELPIDES   You are the sole cause of all our trouble. Why did you bring me from down yonder?

PISTHETÆRUS   To have you with me.

EUELPIDES   Say rather to have me melt into tears.

PISTHETÆRUS   Go to! you are talking nonsense.

EUELPIDES   How so?

PISTHETÆRUS   How will you be able to cry when once your eyes are pecked out?

CHORUS   Io! io! forward to the attack, throw yourselves upon the foe, spill his blood; take to your wings and surround them on all sides. Woe to them! let us get to work with our beaks, let us devour them. Nothing can save them from our wrath, neither the mountain forests, nor the clouds that float in the sky, nor the foaming deep. Come, peck, tear to ribbons. Where is the chief of the cohort? Let him engage the right wing.

EUELPIDES   This is the fatal moment. Where shall I fly to, unfortunate wretch that I am?

PISTHETÆRUS   Stay! stop here!

EUELPIDES   That they may tear me to pieces?

PISTHETÆRUS   And how do you think to escape them?

EUELPIDES   I don't know at all.

PISTHETÆRUS   Come, I will tell you. We must stop and fight them. Let us arm ourselves with these stew-pots.

EUELPIDES   Why with the stew-pots?

PISTHETÆRUS   The owl will not attack us.[1]

EUELPIDES   But do you see all those hooked claws?

PISTHETÆRUS   Seize the spit and pierce the foe on your side.

EUELPIDES   And how about my eyes?

PISTHETÆRUS   Protect them with this dish or this vinegar-pot.

---

[1] An allusion to the Feast of Pots; it was kept at Athens on the third day of the Anthesteria, when all sorts of vegetables were stewed together and offered for the dead to Bacchus and Athené. This Feast was peculiar to Athens. — Hence Pisthetærus thinks that the owl will recognize they are Athenians by seeing the stew-pots, and as he is an Athenian bird, he will not attack them.

EUELPIDES   Oh! what cleverness! what inventive genius! You are a great general, even greater than Nicias,[1] where stratagem is concerned.

CHORUS   Forward, forward, charge with your beaks! Come, no delay. Tear, pluck, strike, flay them, and first of all smash the stew-pot.

EPOPS   Oh, most cruel of all animals, why tear these two men to pieces, why kill them? What have they done to you? They belong to the same tribe, to the same family as my wife.[2]

CHORUS   Are wolves to be spared? Are they not our most mortal foes? So let us punish them.

EPOPS   If they are your foes by nature, they are your friends in heart, and they come here to give you useful advice.

CHORUS   Advice or a useful word from their lips, from them, the enemies of my forebears!

EPOPS   The wise can often profit by the lessons of a foe, for caution is the mother of safety. 'Tis just such a thing as one will not learn from a friend and which an enemy compels you to know. To begin with, 'tis the foe and not the friend that taught cities to build high walls, to equip long vessels of war; and 'tis this knowledge that protects our children, our slaves and our wealth.

CHORUS   Well then, I agree, let us first hear them, for 'tis best; one can even learn something in an enemy's school.

PISTHETÆRUS   Their wrath seems to cool. Draw back a little.

EPOPS   'Tis only justice, and you will thank me later.

CHORUS   Never have we opposed your advice up to now.

PISTHETÆRUS   They are in a more peaceful mood; put down your stew-pot and your two dishes; spit in hand, doing duty for a spear, let us mount guard inside the camp close to the pot and watch in our arsenal closely; for we must not fly.

EUELPIDES   You are right. But where shall we be buried, if we die?

PISTHETÆRUS   In the Ceramicus;[3] for, to get a public funeral, we shall tell the Strategi that we fell at Orneæ,[4] fighting the country's foes.

CHORUS   Return to your ranks and lay down your courage beside your wrath as the Hoplites do. Then let us ask these men who they are, whence they come, and with what intent. Here, Epops, answer me.

EPOPS   Are you calling me? What do you want of me?

---

[1] Nicias, the famous Athenian general. He was joint commander of the Sicilian Expedition.
[2] Procné, the daughter of Pandion, King of Athens.
[3] A space beyond the walls of Athens which contained the gardens of the Academy and the graves of citizens who had died for their country.
[4] A town in Western Argolis, where the Athenians had been recently defeated. There is a somewhat similar word in Greek that signifies *birds*.

CHORUS   Who are they? From what country?

EPOPS   Strangers, who have come from Greece, the land of the wise.

CHORUS   And what fate has led them hither to the land of the birds?

EPOPS   Their love for you and their wish to share your kind of life; to dwell and remain with you always.

CHORUS   Indeed, and what are their plans?

EPOPS   They are wonderful, incredible, unheard of.

CHORUS   Why, do they think to see some advantage that determines them to settle here? Are they hoping with our help to triumph over their foes or to be useful to their friends?

EPOPS   They speak of benefits so great it is impossible either to describe or conceive them; all shall be yours, all that we see here, there, above and below us; this they vouch for.

CHORUS   Are they mad?

EPOPS   They are the sanest people in the world.

CHORUS   Clever men?

EPOPS   The slyest of foxes, cleverness its very self, men of the world, cunning, the cream of knowing folk.

CHORUS   Tell them to speak and speak quickly; why, as I listen to you, I am beside myself with delight.

EPOPS   Here, you there, take all these weapons and hang them up inside close to the fire, near the figure of the god who presides there and under his protection;[1] as for you, address the birds, tell them why I have gathered them together.

PISTHETÆRUS   Not I, by Apollo, unless they agree with me as the little ape of an armourer agreed with his wife, not to bite me, nor pull me by the parts, nor shove things up my . . .

CHORUS   You mean the . . . [Puts finger to bottom.] Oh! be quite at ease.

PISTHETÆRUS   No, I mean my eyes.

CHORUS   Agreed.

PISTHETÆRUS   Swear it.

CHORUS   I swear it and, if I keep my promise, let judges and spectators give me the victory unanimously.

PISTHETÆRUS   It is a bargain.

CHORUS   And if I break my word, may I succeed by one vote only.

HERALD   Hearken, ye people! Hoplites, pick up your weapons and return to your firesides; do not fail to read the decrees of dismissal we have posted.

---

[1]Epops is addressing the two slaves, no doubt Xanthias and Manes, who are mentioned later on.

CHORUS   Man is a truly cunning creature, but nevertheless explain. Perhaps you are going to show me some good way to extend my power, some way that I have not had the wit to find out and which you have discovered. Speak! 'tis to your own interest as well as to mine, for if you secure me some advantage, I will surely share it with you. But what object can have induced you to come among us? Speak boldly, for I shall not break the truce,—until you have told us all.

PISTHETÆRUS   I am bursting with desire to speak; I have already mixed the dough of my address and nothing prevents me from kneading it. . . . Slave! bring the chaplet and water, which you must pour over my hands. Be quick![1]

EUELPIDES   Is it a question of feasting? What does it all mean?

PISTHETÆRUS   By Zeus, no! but I am hunting for fine, tasty words to break down the hardness of their hearts.—I grieve so much for you, who at one time were kings . . .

CHORUS   We kings! Over whom?

PISTHETÆRUS   . . . of all that exists, firstly of me and of this man, even of Zeus himself. Your race is older than Saturn, the Titans and the Earth.

CHORUS   What, older than the Earth!

PISTHETÆRUS   By Phœbus, yes.

CHORUS   By Zeus, but I never knew that before!

PISTHETÆRUS   'Tis because you are ignorant and heedless, and have never read your Æsop. 'Tis he who tells us that the lark was born before all other creatures, indeed before the Earth; his father died of sickness, but the Earth did not exist then; he remained unburied for five days, when the bird in its dilemma decided, for want of a better place, to entomb its father in its own head.

EUELPIDES   So that the lark's father is buried at Cephalæ.[2]

EPOPS   Hence, if we existed before the Earth, before the gods, the kingship belongs to us by right of priority.

EUELPIDES   Undoubtedly, but sharpen your beak well; Zeus won't be in a hurry to hand over his sceptre to the woodpecker.

PISTHETÆRUS   It was not the gods, but the birds, who were formerly the masters and kings over men; of this I have a thousand proofs. First of all, I will point you to the cock, who governed the Persians

---

[1]It was customary, when speaking in public and also at feasts, to wear a chaplet; hence the question Euelpides puts.—The guests wore chaplets of flowers, herbs, and leaves, which had the property of being refreshing.

[2]A deme of Attica. In Greek this word also means *heads*, and hence the pun.

before all other monarchs, before Darius and Megabyzus.[1] 'Tis in memory of his reign that he is called the Persian bird.

EUELPIDES For this reason also, even to-day, he alone of all the birds wears his tiara straight on his head, like the Great King.[2]

PISTHETÆRUS He was so strong, so great, so feared, that even now, on account of his ancient power, everyone jumps out of bed as soon as ever he crows at daybreak. Blacksmiths, potters, tanners, shoemakers, bathmen, corn-dealers, lyre-makers and armourers, all put on their shoes and go to work before it is daylight.

EUELPIDES I can tell you something anent that. 'Twas the cock's fault that I lost a splendid tunic of Phrygian wool. I was at a feast in town, given to celebrate the birth of a child; I had drunk pretty freely and had just fallen asleep, when a cock, I suppose in a greater hurry than the rest, began to crow. I thought it was dawn and set out for Alimos.[3] I had hardly got beyond the walls, when a footpad struck me in the back with his bludgeon; down I went and wanted to shout, but he had already made off with my mantle.

PISTHETÆRUS Formerly also the kite was ruler and king over the Greeks.

EPOPS The Greeks?

PISTHETÆRUS And when he was king, 'twas he who first taught them to fall on their knees before the kites.[4]

EUELPIDES By Zeus! 'tis what I did myself one day on seeing a kite; but at the moment I was on my knees, and leaning backwards[5] with mouth agape, I bolted an obolus and was forced to carry my bag home empty.[6]

PISTHETÆRUS The cuckoo was king of Egypt and of the whole of Phœnicia. When he called out "cuckoo," all the Phœnicians hurried to the fields to reap their wheat and their barley.[7]

---

[1]One of Darius' best generals. After his expedition against the Scythians, this prince gave him the command of the army which he left in Europe. Megabyzus took Perinthos (afterwards called Heraclea) and conquered Thrace.

[2]All Persians wore the tiara, but always on one side; the Great King alone wore it straight on his head.

[3]Noted as the birthplace of Thucydides, a deme of Attica of the tribe of Leontis. Demosthenes tells us it was thirty-five stadia from Athens.

[4]The appearance of the kite in Greece betokened the return of springtime; it was therefore worshipped as a symbol of that season.

[5]To look at the kite, who no doubt was flying high in the sky.

[6]As already shown, the Athenians were addicted to carrying small coins in their mouths.—This obolus was for the purpose of buying flour to fill the bag he was carrying.

[7]In Phœnicia and Egypt the cuckoo makes its appearance about harvest-time.

EUELPIDES   Hence no doubt the proverb, "Cuckoo! cuckoo! go to the fields, ye circumcised."[1]

PISTHETÆRUS   So powerful were the birds, that the kings of Grecian cities, Agamemnon, Menelaus, for instance, carried a bird on the tip of their sceptres, who had his share of all presents.[2]

EUELPIDES   That I didn't know and was much astonished when I saw Priam come upon the stage in the tragedies with a bird, which kept watching Lysicrates[3] to see if he got any present.

PISTHETÆRUS   But the strongest proof of all is, that Zeus, who now reigns, is represented as standing with an eagle on his head as a symbol of his royalty;[4] his daughter has an owl, and Phœbus, as his servant, has a hawk.

EUELPIDES   By Demeter, 'tis well spoken. But what are all these birds doing in heaven?

PISTHETÆRUS   When anyone sacrifices and, according to the rite, offers the entrails to the gods, these birds take their share before Zeus. Formerly men always swore by the birds and never by the gods; even now Lampon[5] swears by the goose, when he wants to lie. . . . Thus 'tis clear that you were great and sacred, but now you are looked upon as slaves, as fools, as Helots; stones are thrown at you as at raving madmen, even in holy places. A crowd of bird-catchers sets snares, traps, limed-twigs and nets of all sorts for you; you are caught, you are sold in heaps and the buyers finger you over to be certain you are fat. Again, if they would but serve you up simply roasted; but they rasp cheese into a mixture of oil, vinegar and laserwort, to which another sweet and greasy sauce is added, and the whole is poured scalding hot over your back, for all the world as if you were diseased meat.

CHORUS   Man, your words have made my heart bleed; I have groaned over the treachery of our fathers, who knew not how to transmit to us the high rank they held from their forefathers. But 'tis a benevolent Genius, a happy Fate, that sends you to us; you shall be our deliverer and I place the destiny of my little ones and my own in your hands with every confidence. But hasten to tell me what must be done; we

---

[1]This was an Egyptian proverb, meaning, *When the cuckoo sings we go harvesting.* Both the Phœnicians and the Egyptians practised circumcision.

[2]The staff, called a sceptre, generally terminated in a piece of carved work, representing a flower, a fruit, and most often a bird.

[3]A general accused of treachery. The bird watches Lysicrates, because, according to Pisthetærus, he had a right to a share of the presents.

[4]It is thus that Phidias represents his Olympian Zeus.

[5]One of the diviners sent to Sybaris (in Magna Græcia, S. Italy) with the Athenian colonists, who rebuilt the town under the new name of Thurium.

should not be worthy to live, if we did not seek to regain our royalty by every possible means.

PISTHETÆRUS   First I advise that the birds gather together in one city and that they build a wall of great bricks, like that at Babylon, round the plains of the air and the whole region of space that divides earth from heaven.

EPOPS   Oh, Cebriones! oh, Porphyrion![1] what a terribly strong place!

PISTHETÆRUS   This, this being well done and completed, you demand back the empire from Zeus; if he will not agree, if he refuses and does not at once confess himself beaten, you declare a sacred war against him and forbid the gods henceforward to pass through your country with lust, as hitherto, for the purpose of fondling their Alcmenas, their Alopés, or their Semelés![2] if they try to pass through, you infibulate them with rings so that they can work no longer. You send another messenger to mankind, who will proclaim to them that the birds are kings, that for the future they must first of all sacrifice to them, and only afterwards to the gods; that it is fitting to appoint to each deity the bird that has most in common with it. For instance, are they sacrificing to Aphrodité, let them at the same time offer barley to the coot; are they immolating a sheep to Posidon, let them consecrate wheat in honour of the duck;[3] is a steer being offered to Heracles, let honey-cakes be dedicated to the gull;[4] is a goat being slain for King Zeus, there is a King-Bird, the wren,[5] to whom the sacrifice of a male gnat is due before Zeus himself even.

EUELPIDES   This notion of an immolated gnat delights me! And now let the great Zeus thunder!

EPOPS   But how will mankind recognize us as gods and not as jays? Us, who have wings and fly?

PISTHETÆRUS   You talk rubbish! Hermes is a god and has wings and flies, and so do many other gods. First of all, Victory flies with golden wings, Eros is undoubtedly winged too, and Iris is compared by

---

[1]As if he were saying, "Oh, gods!" Like Lampon, he swears by the birds, instead of swearing by the gods.—The names of these birds are those of two of the Titans.

[2]Alcmena, wife of Amphitryon, King of Thebes and mother of Heracles.—Semelé, the daughter of Cadmus and Hermioné and mother of Bacchus; both seduced by Zeus.—Alopé, daughter of Cercyon, a robber, who reigned at Eleusis and was conquered by Perseus. Alopé was honoured with Posidon's caresses; by him she had a son named Hippothous, at first brought up by shepherds but who afterwards was restored to the throne of his grandfather by Theseus.

[3]Because water is the duck's domain, as it is that of Posidon.

[4]Because the gull, like Heracles, is voracious.

[5]The Germans still call it Zaunkönig and the French roitelet, both names thus containing the idea of king.

Homer to a timorous dove.[1] If men in their blindness do not recognize you as gods and continue to worship the dwellers in Olympus, then a cloud of sparrows greedy for corn must descend upon their fields and eat up all their seeds; we shall see then if Demeter will mete them out any wheat.

EUELPIDES   By Zeus, she'll take good care she does not, and you will see her inventing a thousand excuses.

PISTHETÆRUS   The crows too will prove your divinity to them by pecking out the eyes of their flocks and of their draught-oxen; and then let Apollo cure them, since he is a physician and is paid for the purpose.[2]

EUELPIDES   Oh! don't do that! Wait first until I have sold my two young bullocks.

PISTHETÆRUS   If on the other hand they recognize that you are God, the principle of life, that you are Earth, Saturn, Posidon, they shall be loaded with benefits.

EPOPS   Name me one of these then.

PISTHETÆRUS   Firstly, the locusts shall not eat up their vine-blossoms; a legion of owls and kestrels will devour them. Moreover, the gnats and the gall-bugs shall no longer ravage the figs; a flock of thrushes shall swallow the whole host down to the very last.

EPOPS   And how shall we give wealth to mankind? This is their strongest passion.

PISTHETÆRUS   When they consult the omens, you will point them to the richest mines, you will reveal the paying ventures to the diviner, and not another shipwreck will happen or sailor perish.

EPOPS   No more shall perish? How is that?

PISTHETÆRUS   When the auguries are examined before starting on a voyage, some bird will not fail to say, "Don't start! there will be a storm," or else, "Go! you will make a most profitable venture."

EUELPIDES   I shall buy a trading-vessel and go to sea. I will not stay with you.

PISTHETÆRUS   You will discover treasures to them, which were buried in former times, for you know them. Do not all men say, "None know where my treasure lies, unless perchance it be some bird."[3]

EUELPIDES   I shall sell my boat and buy a spade to unearth the vessels.

EPOPS   And how are we to give them health, which belongs to the gods?

---

[1]Homer says this of Heré and not of Iris (Iliad, V, 778); it is only another proof that the text of Homer has reached us in a corrupted form, or it may be that Aristophanes was liable, like other people, to occasional mistakes of quotation.

[2]In sacrifices.

[3]An Athenian proverb.

PISTHETÆRUS   If they are happy, is not that the chief thing towards health? The miserable man is never well.

EPOPS   Old Age also dwells in Olympus. How will they get at it? Must they die in early youth?

PISTHETÆRUS   Why, the birds, by Zeus, will add three hundred years to their life.

EPOPS   From whom will they take them?

PISTHETÆRUS   From whom? Why, from themselves. Don't you know the cawing crow lives five times as long as a man?

EUELPIDES   Ah! ah! these are far better kings for us than Zeus!

PISTHETÆRUS   Far better, are they not? And firstly, we shall not have to build them temples of hewn stone, closed with gates of gold; they will dwell amongst the bushes and in the thickets of green oak; the most venerated of birds will have no other temple than the foliage of the olive tree; we shall not go to Delphi or to Ammon to sacrifice;[1] but standing erect in the midst of arbutus and wild olives and holding forth our hands filled with wheat and barley, we shall pray them to admit us to a share of the blessings they enjoy and shall at once obtain them for a few grains of wheat.

CHORUS   Old man, whom I detested, you are now to me the dearest of all; never shall I, if I can help it, fail to follow your advice. Inspirited by your words, I threaten my rivals the gods, and I swear that if you march in alliance with me against the gods and are faithful to our just, loyal and sacred bond, we shall soon have shattered their sceptre. 'Tis our part to undertake the toil, 'tis yours to advise.

EPOPS   By Zeus! 'tis no longer the time to delay and loiter like Nicias;[2] let us act as promptly as possible. . . . In the first place, come, enter my nest built of brushwood and blades of straw, and tell me your names.

PISTHETÆRUS   That is soon done; my name is Pisthetærus.

EPOPS   And his?

PISTHETÆRUS   Euelpides, of the deme of Thria.

EPOPS   Good! and good luck to you.

PISTHETÆRUS   We accept the omen.

EPOPS   Come in here.

PISTHETÆRUS   Very well, 'tis you who lead us and must introduce us.

EPOPS   Come then.

---

[1]A celebrated temple to Zeus in an oasis of Libya.

[2]Nicias was commander, along with Demosthenes, and later on Alcibiades, of the Athenian forces before Syracuse, in the ill-fated Sicilian Expedition, 415–413 B.C. He was much blamed for dilatoriness and indecision.

PISTHETÆRUS   Oh! my god! do come back here. Hi! tell us how we are to follow you. You can fly, but we cannot.

EPOPS   Well, well.

PISTHETÆRUS   Remember Æsop's fables. It is told there, that the fox fared very ill, because he had made an alliance with the eagle.

EPOPS   Be at ease. You shall eat a certain root and wings will grow on your shoulders.

PISTHETÆRUS   Then let us enter. Xanthias and Manes,[1] pick up our baggage.

CHORUS   Hi! Epops! do you hear me?

EPOPS   What's the matter?

CHORUS   Take them off to dine well and call your mate, the melodious Procné, whose songs are worthy of the Muses; she will delight our leisure moments.

PISTHETÆRUS   Oh! I conjure you, accede to their wish; for this delightful bird will leave her rushes at the sound of your voice; for the sake of the gods, let her come here, so that we may contemplate the nightingale.[2]

EPOPS   Let it be as you desire. Come forth, Procné, show yourself to these strangers.

PISTHETÆRUS   Oh! great Zeus! what a beautiful little bird! what a dainty form! what brilliant plumage![3]

EUELPIDES   Do you know how dearly I should like to split her legs for her?

PISTHETÆRUS   She is dazzling all over with gold, like a young girl.[4]

EUELPIDES   Oh! how I should like to kiss her!

PISTHETÆRUS   Why, wretched man, she has two little sharp points on her beak.

EUELPIDES   I would treat her like an egg, the shell of which we remove before eating it; I would take off her mask and then kiss her pretty face.

EPOPS   Let us go in.

PISTHETÆRUS   Lead the way, and may success attend us.

CHORUS   Lovable golden bird, whom I cherish above all others, you, whom I associate with all my songs, nightingale, you have come, you have come, to show yourself to me and to charm me with your notes.

---

[1]Servants of Pisthetærus and Euelpides.

[2]It has already been mentioned that, according to the legend followed by Aristophanes, Procné had been changed into a nightingale and Philomela into a swallow.

[3]The actor, representing Procné, was dressed out as a courtesan, but wore the mask of a bird.

[4]Young unmarried girls wore golden ornaments; the apparel of married women was much simpler.

Come, you, who play spring melodies upon the harmonious flute,[1] lead off our anapæsts.[2]

Weak mortals, chained to the earth, creatures of clay as frail as the foliage of the woods, you unfortunate race, whose life is but darkness, as unreal as a shadow, the illusion of a dream, hearken to us, who are immortal beings, ethereal, ever young and occupied with eternal thoughts, for we shall teach you about all celestial matters; you shall know thoroughly what is the nature of the birds, what the origin of the gods, of the rivers, of Erebus, and Chaos; thanks to us, Prodicus[3] will envy you your knowledge.

At the beginning there was only Chaos, Night, dark Erebus, and deep Tartarus. Earth, the air and heaven had no existence. Firstly, black-winged Night laid a germless egg in the bosom of the infinite deeps of Erebus, and from this, after the revolution of long ages, sprang the graceful Eros with his glittering golden wings, swift as the whirlwinds of the tempest. He mated in deep Tartarus with dark Chaos, winged like himself, and thus hatched forth our race, which was the first to see the light. That of the Immortals did not exist until Eros had brought together all the ingredients of the world, and from their marriage Heaven, Ocean, Earth and the imperishable race of blessed gods sprang into being. Thus our origin is very much older than that of the dwellers in Olympus. We are the offspring of Eros; there are a thousand proofs to show it. We have wings and we lend assistance to lovers. How many handsome youths, who had sworn to remain insensible, have not been vanquished by our power and have yielded themselves to their lovers when almost at the end of their youth, being led away by the gift of a quail, a waterfowl, a goose, or a cock.[4]

And what important services do not the birds render to mortals! First of all, they mark the seasons for them, springtime, winter, and autumn. Does the screaming crane migrate to Libya,—it warns the husbandman to sow, the pilot to take his ease beside his tiller hung up in his dwelling,[5] and Orestes[6] to weave a tunic, so that the rigorous cold may not drive him any more to strip other folk. When the

---

[1]The actor, representing Procné, was a flute-player.
[2]The parabasis.
[3]A sophist of the island of Ceos, a disciple of Protagoras, as celebrated for his knowledge as for his eloquence. The Athenians condemned him to death as a corrupter of youth in 396 B.C.
[4]Lovers were wont to make each other presents of birds. The cock and the goose are mentioned, of course, in jest.
[5]i.e. that it gave notice of the approach of winter, during which season the Ancients did not venture to sea.
[6]A notorious robber.

kite reappears, he tells of the return of spring and of the period when the fleece of the sheep must be clipped. Is the swallow in sight? All hasten to sell their warm tunic and to buy some light clothing. We are your Ammon, Delphi, Dodona, your Phœbus Apollo.[1] Before undertaking anything, whether a business transaction, a marriage, or the purchase of food, you consult the birds by reading the omens, and you give this name of omen[2] to all signs that tell of the future. With you a word is an omen, you call a sneeze an omen, a meeting an omen, an unknown sound an omen, a slave or an ass an omen.[3] Is it not clear that we are a prophetic Apollo to you? If you recognize us as gods, we shall be your divining Muses, through us you will know the winds and the seasons, summer, winter, and the temperate months. We shall not withdraw ourselves to the highest clouds like Zeus, but shall be among you and shall give to you and to your children and the children of your children, health and wealth, long life, peace, youth, laughter, songs and feasts; in short, you will all be so well off, that you will be weary and satiated with enjoyment.

Oh, rustic Muse of such varied note, tio, tio, tio, tiotinx, I sing with you in the groves and on the mountain tops, tio, tio, tio, tio, tiotinx.[4] I pour forth sacred strains from my golden throat in honour of the god Pan,[5] tio, tio, tio, tiotinx, from the top of the thickly leaved ash, and my voice mingles with the mighty choirs who extol Cybelé on the mountain tops,[6] totototototototinx. 'Tis to our concerts that Phrynichus comes to pillage like a bee the ambrosia of his songs, the sweetness of which so charms the ear, tio, tio, tio, tio, tinx.

If there be one of you spectators who wishes to spend the rest of his life quietly among the birds, let him come to us. All that is disgraceful and forbidden by law on earth is on the contrary honourable among us, the birds. For instance, among you 'tis a crime to beat your father, but with us 'tis an estimable deed; it's considered fine to run straight at your father and hit him, saying, "Come, lift your spur if you want to fight."[7] The runaway slave, whom you brand, is only a

---

[1]Meaning, *"We are your oracles."*—Dodona was an oracle in Epirus.—The temple of Zeus there was surrounded by a dense forest, all the trees of which were endowed with the gift of prophecy; both the sacred oaks and the pigeons that lived in them answered the questions of those who came to consult the oracle in pure Greek.
[2]The Greek word for *omen* is the same as that for *bird*.
[3]A satire on the passion of the Greeks for seeing an omen in everything.
[4]An imitation of the nightingale's song.
[5]God of the groves and wilds.
[6]The 'Mother of the Gods'; roaming the mountains, she held dances, always attended by Pan and his accompanying rout of Fauns and Satyrs.
[7]An allusion to cock-fighting; the birds are armed with brazen spurs.

spotted francolin with us.[1] Are you Phrygian like Spintharus?[2] Among us you would be the Phrygian bird, the goldfinch, of the race of Philemon.[3] Are you a slave and a Carian like Execestides? Among us you can create yourself forefathers;[4] you can always find relations. Does the son of Pisias want to betray the gates of the city to the foe? Let him become a partridge, the fitting offspring of his father; among us there is no shame in escaping as cleverly as a partridge.

So the swans on the banks of the Hebrus, tio, tio, tio, tio, tiotinx, mingle their voices to serenade Apollo, tio, tio, tio, tio, tiotinx, flapping their wings the while, tio, tio, tio, tio, tiotinx; their notes reach beyond the clouds of heaven; all the dwellers in the forests stand still with astonishment and delight; a calm rests upon the waters, and the Graces and the choirs in Olympus catch up the strain, tio, tio, tio, tio, tiotinx.

There is nothing more useful nor more pleasant than to have wings. To begin with, just let us suppose a spectator to be dying with hunger and to be weary of the choruses of the tragic poets; if he were winged, he would fly off, go home to dine and come back with his stomach filled. Some Patroclides in urgent need would not have to soil his cloak, but could fly off, satisfy his requirements, and, having recovered his breath, return. If one of you, it matters not who, had adulterous relations and saw the husband of his mistress in the seats of the senators, he might stretch his wings, fly thither, and, having appeased his craving, resume his place. Is it not the most priceless gift of all, to be winged? Look at Diitrephes![5] His wings were only wickerwork ones, and yet he got himself chosen Phylarch and then Hipparch; from being nobody, he has risen to be famous; 'tis now the finest gilded cock of his tribe.

PISTHETÆRUS   Halloa! What's this? By Zeus! I never saw anything so funny in all my life.[6]

EUELPIDES   What makes you laugh?

PISTHETÆRUS   'Tis your bits of wings. D'you know what you look like? Like a goose painted by some dauber-fellow.

EUELPIDES   And you look like a close-shaven blackbird.

---

[1]An allusion to the spots on this bird, which resemble the scars left by a branding iron.
[2]He was of Asiatic origin, but wished to pass for an Athenian.
[3]Or Philamnon, King of Thrace; the Phrygians and the Thracians had a common origin.
[4]The Greek word here is also the name of a little bird.
[5]A basket-maker who had become rich.—The Phylarchs were the headmen of the tribes. They presided at the private assemblies and were charged with the management of the treasury.—The Hipparchs, as the name implies, were the leaders of the cavalry; there were only two of these in the Athenian army.
[6]Pisthetærus and Euelpides now both return with wings.

PISTHETÆRUS 'Tis ourselves asked for this transformation, and, as Æschylus has it, "These are no borrowed feathers, but truly our own."[1]

EPOPS Come now, what must be done?

PISTHETÆRUS First give our city a great and famous name, then sacrifice to the gods.

EUELPIDES I think so too.

EPOPS Let's see. What shall our city be called?

PISTHETÆRUS Will you have a high-sounding Laconian name? Shall we call it Sparta?

EUELPIDES What! call my town Sparta? Why, I would not use esparto for my bed,[2] even though I had nothing but bands of rushes.

PISTHETÆRUS Well then, what name can you suggest?

EUELPIDES Some name borrowed from the clouds, from these lofty regions in which we dwell—in short, some well-known name.

PISTHETÆRUS Do you like Nephelococcygia?[3]

EPOPS Oh! capital! truly 'tis a brilliant thought!

EUELPIDES Is it in Nephelococcygia that all the wealth of Theovenes[4] and most of Aeschines'[5] is?

PISTHETÆRUS No, 'tis rather the plain of Phlegra,[6] where the gods withered the pride of the sons of the Earth with their shafts.

EUELPIDES Oh! what a splendid city! But what god shall be its patron? for whom shall we weave the peplus?[7]

PISTHETÆRUS Why not choose Athené Polias?[8]

EUELPIDES Oh! what a well-ordered town 'twould be to have a female deity armed from head to foot, while Clisthenes[9] was spinning!

PISTHETÆRUS Who then shall guard the Pelargicon?[10]

EPOPS One of ourselves, a bird of Persian strain, who is everywhere proclaimed to be the bravest of all, a true chick of Ares.[11]

---

[1]Meaning, 'tis we who wanted to have these wings.—The verse from Æschylus, quoted here, is taken from 'The Myrmidons,' a tragedy of which only a few fragments remain.

[2]The Greek word signified the city of Sparta, and also a kind of broom used for weaving rough matting, which served for the beds of the very poor.

[3]A fanciful name constructed from a cloud and a cuckoo; thus a city of clouds and cuckoos.—*Wolkenkukelheim* is a clever approximation in German. Cloud-cuckoo-town, perhaps, is the best English equivalent.

[4]He was a boaster nicknamed *smoke*, because he promised a great deal and never kept his word.

[5]A great Athenian orator, second only to Demosthenes.

[6]Because the war of the Titans against the gods was only a fiction of the poets.

[7]A sacred cloth, with which the statue of Athené in the Acropolis was draped.

[8]Meaning, to be patron-goddess of the city. Athené had a temple of this name.

[9]An Athenian effeminate, frequently ridiculed by Aristophanes.

[10]This was the name of the wall surrounding the Acropolis.

[11]i.e. the fighting-cock.

EUELPIDES Oh! noble chick! what a well-chosen god for a rocky home!

PISTHETÆRUS Come! into the air with you to help the workers who are building the wall; carry up rubble, strip yourself to mix the mortar, take up the hod, tumble down the ladder, an [*sic*] you like, post sentinels, keep the fire smouldering beneath the ashes, go round the walls, bell in hand,[1] and go to sleep up there yourself; then despatch two heralds, one to the gods above, the other to mankind on earth and come back here.

EUELPIDES As for yourself, remain here, and may the plague take you for a troublesome fellow!

PISTHETÆRUS Go, friend, go where I send you, for without you my orders cannot be obeyed. For myself, I want to sacrifice to the new god, and I am going to summon the priest who must preside at the ceremony. Slaves! slaves! bring forward the basket and the lustral water.

CHORUS I do as you do, and I wish as you wish, and I implore you to address powerful and solemn prayers to the gods, and in addition to immolate a sheep as a token of our gratitude. Let us sing the Pythian chant in honour of the god, and let Chæris accompany our voices.

PISTHETÆRUS [*to the flute-player*] Enough! but, by Heracles! what is this? Great gods! I have seen many prodigious things, but I never saw a muzzled raven.[2]

EPOPS Priest! 'tis high time! Sacrifice to the new gods.

PRIEST I begin, but where is he with the basket? Pray to the Vesta of the birds, to the kite, who presides over the hearth, and to all the god and goddess-birds who dwell in Olympus.

CHORUS Oh! Hawk, the sacred guardian of Sunium, oh, god of the storks!

PRIEST Pray to the swan of Delos, to Latona the mother of the quails, and to Artemis, the goldfinch.

PISTHETÆRUS 'Tis no longer Artemis Colænis, but Artemis the goldfinch.[3]

PRIEST And to Bacchus, the finch and Cybelé, the ostrich and mother of the gods and mankind.

---

[1]To waken the sentinels, who might else have fallen asleep.—There are several merry contradictions in the various parts of this list of injunctions.

[2]In allusion to the leather strap which flute-players wore to constrict the cheeks and add to the power of the breath. The performer here no doubt wore a raven's mask.

[3]Hellanicus, the Mitylenian historian, tells that this surname of Artemis is derived from Colænus, King of Athens before Cecrops and a descendant of Hermes. In obedience to an oracle he erected a temple to the goddess, invoking her as Artemis Colænis (the Artemis of Colænus).

CHORUS   Oh! sovereign ostrich, Cybelé, the mother of Cleocritus,[1] grant health and safety to the Nephelococcygians as well as to the dwellers in Chios . . .

PISTHETÆRUS   The dwellers in Chios! I am delighted they should be thus mentioned on all occasions.[2]

CHORUS   . . . to the heroes, the birds, to the sons of heroes, to the porphyrion, the pelican, the spoon-bill, the redbreast, the grouse, the peacock, the horned-owl, the teal, the bittern, the heron, the stormy petrel, the fig-pecker, the titmouse . . .

PISTHETÆRUS   Stop! stop! you drive me crazy with your endless list. Why, wretch, to what sacred feast are you inviting the vultures and the sea-eagles? Don't you see that a single kite could easily carry off the lot at once? Begone, you and your fillets and all; I shall know how to complete the sacrifice by myself.

PRIEST   It is imperative that I sing another sacred chant for the rite of the lustral water, and that I invoke the immortals, or at least one of them, provided always that you have some suitable food to offer him; from what I see here, in the shape of gifts, there is naught whatever but horn and hair.

PISTHETÆRUS   Let us address our sacrifices and our prayers to the winged gods.

A POET   Oh, Muse! celebrate happy Nephelococcygia in your hymns.

PISTHETÆRUS   What have we here? Where do you come from, tell me? Who are you?

POET   I am he whose language is sweeter than honey, the zealous slave of the Muses, as Homer has it.

PISTHETÆRUS   You a slave! and yet you wear your hair long?

POET   No, but the fact is all we poets are the assiduous slaves of the Muses, according to Homer.

PISTHETÆRUS   In truth your little cloak is quite holy too through zeal! But, poet, what ill wind drove you here?

POET   I have composed verses in honour of your Nephelococcygia, a host of splendid dithyrambs and parthenians,[3] worthy of Simonides himself.

PISTHETÆRUS   And when did you compose them? How long since?

POET   Oh! 'tis long, aye, very long, that I have sung in honour of this city.

---

[1] This Cleocritus was long-necked and strutted like an ostrich.
[2] The Chians were the most faithful allies of Athens, and hence their name was always mentioned in prayers, decrees, etc.
[3] Verses sung by maidens.

PISTHETÆRUS   But I am only celebrating its foundation with this sacrifice;[1] I have only just named it, as is done with little babies.

POET   "Just as the chargers fly with the speed of the wind, so does the voice of the Muses take its flight. Oh! thou noble founder of the town of Ætna,[2] thou, whose name recalls the holy sacrifices, make us such gift as thy generous heart shall suggest.

PISTHETÆRUS   He will drive us silly if we do not get rid of him by some present. Here! you, who have a fur as well as your tunic, take it off and give it to this clever poet. Come, take this fur; you look to me to be shivering with cold.

POET   My Muse will gladly accept this gift; but engrave these verses of Pindar's on your mind.

PISTHETÆRUS   Oh! what a pest! 'Tis impossible then to be rid of him.

POET   "Straton wanders among the Scythian nomads, but has no linen garment. He is sad at only wearing an animal's pelt and no tunic." Do you conceive my bent?

PISTHETÆRUS   I understand that you want me to offer you a tunic. Hi! you [to EUELPIDES], take off yours; we must help the poet. . . . Come, you, take it and begone.

POET   I am going, and these are the verses that I address to this city: "Phœbus of the golden throne, celebrate this shivery, freezing city; I have travelled through fruitful and snow-covered plains. Tralala! Tralala!"[3]

PISTHETÆRUS   What are you chanting us about frosts? Thanks to the tunic, you no longer fear them. Ah! by Zeus! I could not have believed this cursed fellow could so soon have learnt the way to our city. Come, priest, take the lustral water and circle the altar.

PRIEST   Let all keep silence!

A PROPHET   Let not the goat be sacrificed.[4]

PISTHETÆRUS   Who are you?

PROPHET   Who am I? A prophet.

PISTHETÆRUS   Get you gone.

PROPHET   Wretched man, insult not sacred things. For there is an oracle of Bacis, which exactly applies to Nephelococcygia.

PISTHETÆRUS   Why did you not reveal it to me before I founded my city?

PROPHET   The divine spirit was against it.

PISTHETÆRUS   Well, 'tis best to know the terms of the oracle.

---

[1]This ceremony took place on the tenth day after birth, and may be styled the pagan baptism.
[2]Hiero, tyrant of Syracuse.—This passage is borrowed from Pindar.
[3]A parody of poetic pathos, not to say bathos.
[4]Which the priest was preparing to sacrifice.

PROPHET   "But when the wolves and the white crows shall dwell together between Corinth and Sicyon. . . ."

PISTHETÆRUS   But how do the Corinthians concern me?

PROPHET   'Tis the regions of the air that Bacis indicated in this manner. "They must first sacrifice a white-fleeced goat to Pandora, and give the prophet, who first reveals my words, a good cloak and new sandals."

PISTHETÆRUS   Are the sandals there?

PROPHET   Read. "And besides this a goblet of wine and a good share of the entrails of the victim."

PISTHETÆRUS   Of the entrails—is it so written?

PROPHET   Read. "If you do as I command, divine youth, you shall be an eagle among the clouds; if not, you shall be neither turtle-dove, nor eagle, nor woodpecker."

PISTHETÆRUS   Is all that there?

PROPHET   Read.

PISTHETÆRUS   This oracle in no sort of way resembles the one Apollo dictated to me: "If an impostor comes without invitation to annoy you during the sacrifice and to demand a share of the victim, apply a stout stick to his ribs."

PROPHET   You are drivelling.

PISTHETÆRUS   "And don't spare him, were he an eagle from out of the clouds, were it Lampon himself[1] or the great Diopithes."[2]

PROPHET   Is all that there?

PISTHETÆRUS   Here, read it yourself, and go and hang yourself.

CHORUS   Oh! unfortunate wretch that I am.

PISTHETÆRUS   Away with you, and take your prophecies elsewhere.

METON[3]   I have come to you.

PISTHETÆRUS   Yet another pest. What have you come to do? What's your plan? What's the purpose of your journey? Why these splendid buskins?

METON   I want to survey the plains of the air for you and to parcel them into lots.

PISTHETÆRUS   In the name of the gods, who are you?

METON   Who am I? Meton, known throughout Greece and at Colonus.[4]

---

[1]Noted Athenian diviner, who, when the power was still shared between Thucydides and Pericles, predicted that it would soon be centred in the hands of the latter; his ground for this prophecy was the sight of a ram with a single horn.

[2]No doubt another Athenian diviner, and possibly the same person whom Aristophanes names in 'The Knights' and 'The Wasps' as being a thief.

[3]A celebrated geometrician and astronomer.

[4]A deme contiguous to Athens.

PISTHETÆRUS What are these things?

METON Tools for measuring the air. In truth, the spaces in the air have precisely the form of a furnace. With this bent ruler I draw a line from top to bottom; from one of its points I describe a circle with the compass. Do you understand?

PISTHETÆRUS Not the very least.

METON With the straight ruler I set to work to inscribe a square within this circle; in its centre will be the market-place, into which all the straight streets will lead, converging to this centre like a star, which, although only orbicular, sends forth its rays in a straight line from all sides.

PISTHETÆRUS Meton, you new Thales[1] . . .

METON What d'you want with me?

PISTHETÆRUS I want to give you a proof of my friendship. Use your legs.

METON Why, what have I to fear?

PISTHETÆRUS 'Tis the same here as in Sparta. Strangers are driven away, and blows rain down as thick as hail.

METON Is there sedition in your city?

PISTHETÆRUS No, certainly not.

METON What's wrong then?

PISTHETÆRUS We are agreed to sweep all quacks and impostors far from our borders.

METON Then I'm off.

PISTHETÆRUS I fear me 'tis too late. The thunder growls already.

[*Beats him.*]

METON Oh, woe! oh, woe!

PISTHETÆRUS I warned you. Now, be off, and do your surveying somewhere else.   [METON *takes to his heels.*]

AN INSPECTOR Where are the Proxeni?[2]

PISTHETÆRUS Who is this Sardanapalus?[3]

INSPECTOR I have been appointed by lot to come to Nephelococcygia as inspector.[4]

PISTHETÆRUS An inspector! and who sends you here, you rascal?

INSPECTOR A decree of Taleas.[5]

---

[1]Thales was no less famous as a geometrician than he was as a sage.

[2]Officers of Athens, whose duty was to protect strangers who came on political or other business, and see to their interests generally.

[3]He addresses the inspector thus because of the royal and magnificent manners he assumes.

[4]Magistrates appointed to inspect the tributary towns.

[5]A much-despised citizen, already mentioned. He ironically supposes him invested with the powers of an Archon, which ordinarily were entrusted only to men of good repute.

PISTHETÆRUS   Will you just pocket your salary, do nothing, and be off?

INSPECTOR   I' faith! that I will; I am urgently needed to be at Athens to attend the assembly; for I am charged with the interests of Pharnaces.[1]

PISTHETÆRUS   Take it then, and be off. See, here is your salary.

[Beats him.]

INSPECTOR   What does this mean?

PISTHETÆRUS   'Tis the assembly where you have to defend Pharnaces.

INSPECTOR   You shall testify that they dare to strike me, the inspector.

PISTHETÆRUS   Are you not going to clear out with your urns? 'Tis not to be believed; they send us inspectors before we have so much as paid sacrifice to the gods.

A DEALER IN DECREES   "If the Nephelococcygian does wrong to the Athenian . . ."

PISTHETÆRUS   Now whatever are these cursed parchments?

DEALER IN DECREES   I am a dealer in decrees, and I have come here to sell you the new laws.

PISTHETÆRUS   Which?

DEALER IN DEGREES   "The Nephelococcygians shall adopt the same weights, measures and decrees as the Olophyxians."[2]

PISTHETÆRUS   And you shall soon be imitating the Ototyxians.

[Beats him.]

DEALER IN DECREES   Hullo! what are you doing?

PISTHETÆRUS   Now will you be off with your decrees? For I am going to let *you* see some severe ones.

INSPECTOR *[returning]*   I summon Pisthetærus for outrage for the month of Munychion.[3]

PISTHETÆRUS   Ha! my friend! are you still there?

DEALER IN DECREES   "Should anyone drive away the magistrates and not receive them, according to the decree duly posted . . ."

PISTHETÆRUS   What! rascal! you are there too?

INSPECTOR   Woe to you! I'll have you condemned to a fine of ten thousand drachmæ.

---

[1] A Persian satrap.—An allusion to certain orators, who, bribed with Asiatic gold, had often defended the interests of the foe in the Public Assembly.

[2] A Macedonian people in the peninsula of Chalcidicé. This name is chosen because of its similarity to the Greek word *to groan*. It is from another Greek verb meaning the same thing, that Pisthetærus coins the name of Ototyxians, i.e. groaners, because he is about to beat the dealer.—The mother-country had the right to impose any law it chose upon its colonies.

[3] Corresponding to our month of April.

PISTHETÆRUS And I'll smash your urns.[1]

INSPECTOR Do you recall that evening when you stooled against the column where the decrees are posted?

PISTHETÆRUS Here! here! let him be seized. [THE INSPECTOR *runs off.*] Well! don't you want to stop any longer?

PRIEST Let us get indoors as quick as possible; we will sacrifice the goat inside.[2]

CHORUS Henceforth it is to me that mortals must address their sacrifices and their prayers. Nothing escapes my sight nor my might. My glance embraces the universe, I preserve the fruit in the flower by destroying the thousand kinds of voracious insects the soil produces, which attack the trees and feed on the germ when it has scarcely formed in the calyx; I destroy those who ravage the balmy terrace gardens like a deadly plague; all these gnawing crawling creatures perish beneath the lash of my wing. I hear it proclaimed everywhere: "A talent for him who shall kill Diagoras of Melos,[3] and a talent for him who destroys one of the dead tyrants."[4] We likewise wish to make our proclamation: "A talent to him among you who shall kill Philocrates, the Strouthian;[5] four, if he brings him to us alive. For this Philocrates skewers the finches together and sells them at the rate of an obolus for seven. He tortures the thrushes by blowing them out, so that they may look bigger, sticks their own feathers into the nostrils of blackbirds, and collects pigeons, which he shuts up and forces them, fastened in a net, to decoy others." That is what we wish to proclaim. And if anyone is keeping birds shut up in his yard, let him hasten to let them loose; those who disobey shall be seized by the birds and we shall put them in chains, so that in their turn they may decoy other men.

Happy indeed is the race of winged birds who need no cloak in winter! Neither do I fear the relentless rays of the fiery dogdays; when the divine grasshopper, intoxicated with the sunlight, when noon is

[1]Which the inspector had brought with him for the purpose of inaugurating the assemblies of the people or some tribunal.
[2]So that the sacrifices might no longer be interrupted.
[3]A disciple of Democrites; he passed over from superstition to atheism. The injustice and perversity of mankind led him to deny the existence of the gods, to lay bare the mysteries and to break the idols. The Athenians had put a price on his head, so he left Greece and perished soon afterwards in a storm at sea.
[4]By this jest Aristophanes means to imply that tyranny is dead, and that no one aspires to despotic power, though this silly accusation was constantly being raised by the demagogues and always favourably received by the populace.
[5]A poulterer.—Strouthian, used in jest to designate him, as if from the name of his 'deme,' is derived from the Greek word for *sparrow*. The birds' foe is thus grotesquely furnished with an ornithological surname.

burning the ground, is breaking out into shrill melody, my home is beneath the foliage in the flowery meadows. I winter in deep caverns, where I frolic with the mountain nymphs, while in spring I despoil the gardens of the Graces and gather the white, virgin berry on the myrtle bushes. I want now to speak to the judges about the prize they are going to award; if they are favourable to us, we will load them with benefits far greater than those Paris[1] received. Firstly, the owls of Laurium,[2] which every judge desires above all things, shall never be wanting to you; you shall see them homing with you, building their nests in your money-bags and laying coins. Besides, you shall be housed like the gods, for we shall erect gables[3] over your dwellings; if you hold some public post and want to do a little pilfering, we will give you the sharp claws of a hawk. Are you dining in town, we will provide you with crops.[4] But, if your award is against us, don't fail to have metal covers fashioned for yourselves, like those they place over statues;[5] else, look out! for the day you wear a white tunic all the birds will soil it with their droppings.

PISTHETÆRUS   Birds! the sacrifice is propitious. But I see no messenger coming from the wall to tell us what is happening. Ah! here comes one running himself out of breath as though he were running the Olympic stadium.

MESSENGER   Where, where is he? Where, where, where is he? Where, where, where is he? Where is Pisthetærus, our leader?

PISTHETÆRUS   Here am I.

MESSENGER   The wall is finished.

PISTHETÆRUS   That's good news.

MESSENGER   'Tis a most beautiful, a most magnificent work of art. The wall is so broad, that Proxenides, the Braggartian, and Theogenes could pass each other in their chariots, even if they were drawn by steeds as big as the Trojan horse.

PISTHETÆRUS   'Tis wonderful!

MESSENGER   Its length is one hundred stadia; I measured it myself.

---

[1]From Aphrodité (Venus), to whom he had awarded the apple, prize of beauty, in the contest of the "goddesses three."

[2]Laurium was an Athenian deme at the extremity of the Attic peninsula containing valuable silver mines, the revenues of which were largely employed in the maintenance of the fleet and payment of the crews. The "owls of Laurium," of course, mean pieces of money; the Athenian coinage was stamped with a representation of an owl, the bird of Athené.

[3]A pun, impossible to keep in English, on the two meanings of this word in Greek, which signifies both an eagle and the gable of a house or pediment of a temple.

[4]That is, birds' crops, into which they could stow away plenty of good things.

[5]The Ancients appear to have placed metal discs over statues standing in the open air, to save them from injury from the weather, etc.

PISTHETÆRUS   A decent length, by Posidon! And who built such a wall?

MESSENGER   Birds—birds only; they had neither Egyptian brick-maker, nor stonemason, nor carpenter; the birds did it all themselves; I could hardly believe my eyes. Thirty thousand cranes came from Libya with a supply of stones,[1] intended for the foundations. The water-rails chiselled them with their beaks. Ten thousand storks were busy making bricks; plovers and other water fowl carried water into the air.

PISTHETÆRUS   And who carried the mortar?

MESSENGER   Herons, in hods.

PISTHETÆRUS   But how could they put the mortar into hods?

MESSENGER   Oh! 'twas a truly clever invention; the geese used their feet like spades; they buried them in the pile of mortar and then emptied them into the hods.

PISTHETÆRUS   Ah! to what use cannot feet be put?[2]

MESSENGER   You should have seen how eagerly the ducks carried bricks. To complete the tale, the swallows came flying to the work, their beaks full of mortar and their trowel on their back, just the way little children are carried.

PISTHETÆRUS   Who would want paid servants after this? But, tell me, who did the woodwork?

MESSENGER   Birds again, and clever carpenters too, the pelicans, for they squared up the gates with their beaks in such a fashion that one would have thought they were using axes; the noise was just like a dockyard. Now the whole wall is tight everywhere, securely bolted and well guarded; it is patrolled, bell in hand; the sentinels stand everywhere and beacons burn on the towers. But I must run off to clean myself; the rest is your business.

CHORUS   Well! what do you say to it? Are you not astonished at the wall being completed so quickly?

PISTHETÆRUS   By the gods, yes, and with good reason. 'Tis really not to be believed. But here comes another messenger from the wall to bring us some further news! What a fighting look he has!

SECOND MESSENGER   Oh! oh! oh! oh! oh! oh!

PISTHETÆRUS   What's the matter?

SECOND MESSENGER   A horrible outrage has occurred; a god sent by Zeus has passed through our gates and has penetrated the realms of the air without the knowledge of the jays, who are on guard in the daytime.

---

[1]So as not to be carried away by the wind when crossing the sea, cranes are popularly supposed to ballast themselves with stones, which they carry in their beaks.

[2]Pisthetærus modifies the Greek proverbial saying, "To what use cannot hands be put?"

PISTHETÆRUS   'Tis an unworthy and criminal deed. What god was it?

SECOND MESSENGER   We don't know that. All we know is, that he has got wings.

PISTHETÆRUS   Why were not guards sent against him at once?

SECOND MESSENGER   We have despatched thirty thousand hawks of the legion of mounted archers.[1] All the hook-clawed birds are moving against him, the kestrel, the buzzard, the vulture, the great-horned owl; they cleave the air, so that it resounds with the flapping of their wings; they are looking everywhere for the god, who cannot be far away; indeed, if I mistake not, he is coming from yonder side.

PISTHETÆRUS   All arm themselves with slings and bows! This way, all our soldiers; shoot and strike! Some one give me a sling!

CHORUS   War, a terrible war is breaking out between us and the gods! Come, let each one guard the Air, the son of Erebus,[2] in which the clouds float. Take care no immortal enters it without your knowledge. Scan all sides with your glance. Hark! methinks I can hear the rustle of the swift wings of a god from heaven.

PISTHETÆRUS   Hi! you woman! where are you flying to? Halt, don't stir! keep motionless! not a beat of your wing!—Who are you and from what country? You must say whence you come.[3]

IRIS   I come from the abode of the Olympian gods.

PISTHETÆRUS   What's your name, ship or cap?[4]

IRIS   I am swift Iris.

PISTHETÆRUS   Paralus or Salaminia?[5]

IRIS   What do you mean?

PISTHETÆRUS   Let a buzzard rush at her and seize her.[6]

IRIS   Seize me! But what do all these insults betoken?

PISTHETÆRUS   Woe to you!

IRIS   'Tis incomprehensible.

PISTHETÆRUS   By which gate did you pass through the wall, wretched woman?

IRIS   By which gate? Why, great gods, I don't know.

PISTHETÆRUS   You hear how she holds us in derision. Did you present

---

[1]A corps of Athenian cavalry was so named.

[2]Chaos, Night, Tartarus, and Erebus alone existed in the beginning; Eros was born from Night and Erebus, and he wedded Chaos and begot Earth, Air, and Heaven; so runs the fable.

[3]Iris appears from the top of the stage and arrests her flight in mid-career.

[4]Ship, because of her wings, which resemble oars; cap, because she no doubt wore the head-dress (as a messenger of the gods) with which Hermes is generally depicted.

[5]The names of the two sacred galleys which carried Athenian officials on State business.

[6]A buzzard is named in order to raise a laugh, the Greek name also meaning, etymologically, provided with three testicles, vigorous in love.

yourself to the officers in command of the jays? You don't answer. Have you a permit, bearing the seal of the storks?

IRIS Am I awake?

PISTHETÆRUS Did you get one?

IRIS Are you mad?

PISTHETÆRUS No head-bird gave you a safe-conduct?

IRIS A safe-conduct to me, you poor fool!

PISTHETÆRUS Ah! and so you slipped into this city on the sly and into these realms of air-land that don't belong to you.

IRIS And what other road can the gods travel?

PISTHETÆRUS By Zeus! I know nothing about that, not I. But they won't pass this way. And you still dare to complain! Why, if you were treated according to your deserts, no Iris would ever have more justly suffered death.

IRIS I am immortal.

PISTHETÆRUS You would have died nevertheless.—Oh! 'twould be truly intolerable! What! should the universe obey us and the gods alone continue their insolence and not understand that they must submit to the law of the strongest in their due turn? But tell me, where are you flying to?

IRIS I? The messenger of Zeus to mankind, I am going to tell them to sacrifice sheep and oxen on the altars and to fill their streets with the rich smoke of burning fat.

PISTHETÆRUS Of which gods are you speaking?

IRIS Of which? Why, of ourselves, the gods of heaven.

PISTHETÆRUS You, gods?

IRIS Are there others then?

PISTHETÆRUS Men now adore the birds as gods, and 'tis to them, by Zeus, that they must offer sacrifices, and not to Zeus at all!

IRIS Oh! fool! fool! Rouse not the wrath of the gods, for 'tis terrible indeed. Armed with the brand of Zeus, Justice would annihilate your race; the lightning would strike you as it did Lycimnius and consume both your body and the porticos of your palace.[1]

PISTHETÆRUS Here! that's enough tall talk. Just you listen and keep quiet! Do you take me for a Lydian or a Phrygian[2] and think to frighten me with your big words? Know, that if Zeus worries me again, I shall go at the head of my eagles, who are armed with lightning, and reduce his dwelling and that of Amphion to cinders.[3] I shall send more than six hundred porphyrions clothed in leopards'

---

[1] Iris' reply is a parody of the tragic style.—'Lycimnius' is the title of a tragedy by Euripides, which is about a ship that is struck by lightning.

[2] i.e. for a poltroon, like the slaves, most of whom came to Athens from these countries.

[3] A parody of a passage in the lost tragedy of 'Niobé' of Æschylus.

skins[1] up to heaven against him; and formerly a single Porphyrion gave him enough to do. As for you, his messenger, if you annoy me, I shall begin by stretching your legs asunder and so conduct myself, Iris though you be, that despite my age, you will be astonished. I will show you something that will make you three times over.

IRIS   May you perish, you wretch, you and your infamous words!

PISTHETÆRUS   Won't you be off quickly? Come, stretch your wings or look out for squalls!

IRIS   If my father does not punish you for your insults . . .

PISTHETÆRUS   Ha! . . . but just you be off elsewhere to roast younger folk than us with your lightning.

CHORUS   We forbid the gods, the sons of Zeus, to pass through our city and the mortals to send them the smoke of their sacrifices by this road.

PISTHETÆRUS   'Tis odd that the messenger we sent to the mortals has never returned.

HERALD   Oh! blessed Pisthetærus, very wise, very illustrious, very gracious, thrice happy, very . . . Come, prompt me, somebody, do.

PISTHETÆRUS   Get to your story!

HERALD   All peoples are filled with admiration for your wisdom, and they award you this golden crown.

PISTHETÆRUS   I accept it. But tell me, why do the people admire me?

HERALD   Oh you, who have founded so illustrious a city in the air, you know not in what esteem men hold you and how many there are who burn with desire to dwell in it. Before your city was built, all men had a mania for Sparta; long hair and fasting were held in honour, men went dirty like Socrates and carried staves. Now all is changed. Firstly, as soon as 'tis dawn, they all spring out of bed together to go and seek their food, the same as you do; then they fly off towards the notices and finally devour the decrees. The bird-madness is so clear, that many actually bear the names of birds. There is a halting victualler, who styles himself the partridge; Menippus calls himself the swallow; Opontius the one-eyed crow; Philocles the lark; Theogenes the fox-goose; Lycurgus the ibis; Chærephon the bat; Syracosius the magpie; Midias the quail;[2] indeed he looks like a quail that has been hit heavily over the head. Out of love for the birds they repeat all the songs which concern the swallow, the teal,

---

[1]Because this bird has a spotted plumage.—Porphyrion is also the name of one of the Titans who tried to storm heaven.

[2]All these surnames bore some relation to the character or the build of the individual to whom the poet applies them.—Chærephon, Socrates' disciple, was of white and ashen hue.—Opontius was one-eyed.—Syracosius was a braggart.—Midias had a passion for quail-fights, and, besides, resembled that bird physically.

the goose or the pigeon; in each verse you see wings, or at all events
a few feathers. This is what is happening down there. Finally, there
are more than ten thousand folk who are coming here from earth to
ask you for feathers and hooked claws; so, mind you supply yourself
with wings for the immigrants.

PISTHETÆRUS   Ah! by Zeus, 'tis not the time for idling. Go as quick as
possible and fill every hamper, every basket you can find with wings.
Manes[1] will bring them to me outside the walls, where I will welcome those who present themselves.

CHORUS   This town will soon be inhabited by a crowd of men.

PISTHETÆRUS   If fortune favours us.

CHORUS   Folk are more and more delighted with it.

PISTHETÆRUS   Come, hurry up and bring them along.

CHORUS   Will not man find here everything that can please him—
wisdom, love, the divine Graces, the sweet face of gentle peace?

PISTHETÆRUS   Oh! you lazy servant! won't you hurry yourself?

CHORUS   Let a basket of wings be brought speedily. Come, beat him
as I do, and put some life into him; he is as lazy as an ass.

PISTHETÆRUS   Aye, Manes is a great craven.

CHORUS   Begin by putting this heap of wings in order; divide them in
three parts according to the birds from whom they came; the singing,
the prophetic[2] and the aquatic birds; then you must take care to dis-
tribute them to the men according to their character.

PISTHETÆRUS [to MANES]   Oh! by the kestrels! I can keep my hands
off you no longer; you are too slow and lazy altogether.

A PARRICIDE[3]   Oh! might I but become an eagle, who soars in the
skies! Oh! might I fly above the azure waves of the barren sea![4]

PISTHETÆRUS   Ha! 'twould seem the news was true; I hear someone
coming who talks of wings.

PARRICIDE   Nothing is more charming than to fly; I burn with desire
to live under the same laws as the birds; I am bird-mad and fly towards you, for I want to live with you and to obey your laws.

PISTHETÆRUS   Which laws? The birds have many laws.

PARRICIDE   All of them; but the one that pleases me most is, that
among the birds it is considered a fine thing to peck and strangle
one's father.

PISTHETÆRUS   Aye, by Zeus! according to us, he who dares to strike
his father, while still a chick, is a brave fellow.

---

[1]Pisthetærus' servant, already mentioned.
[2]From the inspection of which auguries were taken, e.g. the eagles, the vultures, the
crows.
[3]Or rather, a young man who contemplated parricide.
[4]A parody of verses in Sophocles' 'Œnomaus.'

Aristophanes

PARRICIDE   And therefore I want to dwell here, for I want to strangle my father and inherit his wealth.

PISTHETÆRUS   But we have also an ancient law written in the code of the storks, which runs thus, "When the stork father has reared his young and has taught them to fly, the young must in their turn support the father."

PARRICIDE   'Tis hardly worth while coming all this distance to be compelled to keep my father!

PISTHETÆRUS   No, no, young friend, since you have come to us with such willingness, I am going to give you these black wings, as though you were an orphan bird; furthermore, some good advice, that I received myself in infancy. Don't strike your father, but take these wings in one hand and these spurs in the other; imagine you have a cock's crest on your head and go and mount guard and fight; live on your pay and respect your father's life. You're a gallant fellow! Very well, then! Fly to Thrace and fight.[1]

PARRICIDE   By Bacchus! 'Tis well spoken; I will follow your counsel.

PISTHETÆRUS   'Tis acting wisely, by Zeus.

CINESIAS[2]   "On my light pinions I soar off to Olympus; in its capricious flight my Muse flutters along the thousand paths of poetry in turn . . ."

PISTHETÆRUS   This is a fellow will need a whole shipload of wings.

CINESIAS   ". . . and being fearless and vigorous, it is seeking fresh outlet."

PISTHETÆRUS   Welcome, Cinesias, you lime-wood man![3] Why have you come here a-twisting your game leg in circles?

CINESIAS   "I want to become a bird, a tuneful nightingale."

PISTHETÆRUS   Enough of that sort of ditty. Tell me what you want.

CINESIAS   Give me wings and I will fly into the topmost airs to gather fresh songs in the clouds, in the midst of the vapours and the fleecy snow.

PISTHETÆRUS   Gather songs in the clouds?

CINESIAS   'Tis on them the whole of our latter-day art depends. The most brilliant dithyrambs are those that flap their wings in void space and are clothed in mist and dense obscurity. To appreciate this, just listen.

PISTHETÆRUS   Oh! no, no, no!

CINESIAS   By Hermes! but indeed you shall. "I shall travel through

---

[1]The Athenians were then besieging Amphipolis in the Thracian Chalcidicé.
[2]There was a real Cinesias—a dithyrambic poet, born at Thebes.
[3]One scholarly interpretation has it that Cinesias, who was tall and slight of build, wore a kind of corset of lime-wood to support his waist.

thine ethereal empire like a winged bird, who cleaveth space with
his long neck . . ."
PISTHETÆRUS   Stop! easy all, I say![1]
CINESIAS   ". . . as I soar over the seas, carried by the breath of the
winds . . ."
PISTHETÆRUS   By Zeus! but I'll cut your breath short.
CINESIAS   ". . . now rushing along the tracks of Notus, now nearing
Boreas across the infinite wastes of the ether." [PISTHETÆRUS *beats
him*.] Ah! old man, that's a pretty and clever idea truly!
PISTHETÆRUS   What! are you not delighted to be cleaving the air?[2]
CINESIAS   To treat a dithyrambic poet, for whom the tribes dispute
with each other, in this style![3]
PISTHETÆRUS   Will you stay with us and form a chorus of winged
birds as slender as Leotrophides[4] for the Cecropid tribe?
CINESIAS   You are making game of me, 'tis clear; but know that I shall
never leave you in peace if I do not have wings wherewith to traverse
the air.
AN INFORMER   What are these birds with downy feathers, who look so
pitiable to me? Tell me, oh swallow with the long dappled wings.[5]
PISTHETÆRUS   Oh! but 'tis a perfect invasion that threatens us. Here
comes another of them, humming along.
INFORMER   Swallow with the long dappled wings, once more I sum-
mon you.
PISTHETÆRUS   It's his cloak I believe he's addressing; 'faith, it stands in
great need of the swallows' return.[6]
INFORMER   Where is he who gives out wings to all comers?
PISTHETÆRUS   'Tis I, but you must tell me for what purpose you want
them.
INFORMER   Ask no questions. I want wings, and wings I must have.
PISTHETÆRUS   Do you want to fly straight to Pellené?[7]

[1]The Greek word used here was the word of command employed to stop the rowers.
[2]Cinesias makes a bound each time that Pisthetærus strikes him.
[3]The tribes of Athens, or rather the rich citizens belonging to them, were wont on feast-
days to give representations of dithyrambic choruses as well as of tragedies and
comedies.
[4]Another dithyrambic poet, a man of extreme leanness.
[5]A parody of a hemistich from 'Alcæus.'—The informer is dissatisfied at only seeing
birds of sombre plumage and poor appearance. He would have preferred to denounce
the rich.
[6]The informer was clothed with a ragged cloak, the tatters of which hung down like
wings, in fact, a cloak that could not protect him from the cold and must have made
him long for the swallows' return, i.e. the spring.
[7]A town in Achaia, where woollen cloaks were made.

INFORMER   I? Why, I am an accuser of the islands,[1] an informer . . .

PISTHETÆRUS   A fine trade, truly!

INFORMER   . . . a hatcher of lawsuits. Hence I have great need of wings to prowl round the cities and drag them before justice.

PISTHETÆRUS   Would you do this better if you had wings?

INFORMER   No, but I should no longer fear the pirates; I should return with the cranes, loaded with a supply of lawsuits by way of ballast.

PISTHETÆRUS   So it seems, despite all your youthful vigour, you make it your trade to denounce strangers?

INFORMER   Well, and why not? I don't know how to dig.

PISTHETÆRUS   But, by Zeus! there are honest ways of gaining a living at your age without all this infamous trickery.

INFORMER   My friend, I am asking you for wings, not for words.

PISTHETÆRUS   'Tis just my words that give you wings.

INFORMER   And how can you give a man wings with your words?

PISTHETÆRUS   'Tis thus that all first start.

INFORMER   All?

PISTHETÆRUS   Have you not often heard the father say to young men in the barbers' shops, "It's astonishing how Diitrephes' advice has made my son fly to horse-riding."—"Mine," says another, "has flown towards tragic poetry on the wings of his imagination."

INFORMER   So that words give wings?

PISTHETÆRUS   Undoubtedly; words give wings to the mind and make a man soar to heaven. Thus I hope that my wise words will give you wings to fly to some less degrading trade.

INFORMER   But I do not want to.

PISTHETÆRUS   What do you reckon on doing then?

INFORMER   I won't belie my breeding; from generation to generation we have lived by informing. Quick, therefore, give me quickly some light, swift hawk or kestrel wings, so that I may summon the islanders, sustain the accusation here, and haste back there again on flying pinions.

PISTHETÆRUS   I see. In this way the stranger will be condemned even before he appears.

INFORMER   That's just it.

PISTHETÆRUS   And while he is on his way here by sea, you will be flying to the islands to despoil him of his property.

INFORMER   You've hit it, precisely; I must whirl hither and thither like a perfect humming-top.

---

[1]His trade was to accuse the rich citizens of the subject islands, and drag them before the Athenian courts; he explains later the special advantages of this branch of the informer's business.

PISTHETÆRUS I catch the idea. Wait, i' faith, I've got some fine Corcyræan wings.[1] How do you like them?

INFORMER Oh! woe is me! Why, 'tis a whip!

PISTHETÆRUS No, no; these are the wings, I tell you, that set the top a-spinning.

INFORMER Oh! oh! oh!

PISTHETÆRUS Take your flight, clear off, you miserable cur, or you will soon see what comes of quibbling and lying. Come, let us gather up our wings and withdraw.

CHORUS In my ethereal flights I have seen many things new and strange and wondrous beyond belief. There is a tree called Cleonymus belonging to an unknown species; it has no heart, is good for nothing and is as tall as it is cowardly. In springtime it shoots forth calumnies instead of buds and in autumn it strews the ground with bucklers in place of leaves.[2]

Far away in the regions of darkness, where no ray of light ever enters, there is a country, where men sit at the table of the heroes and dwell with them always—save always in the evening. Should any mortal meet the hero Orestes at night, he would soon be stripped and covered with blows from head to foot.[3]

PROMETHEUS Ah! by the gods! if only Zeus does not espy me! Where is Pisthetærus?

PISTHETÆRUS Ha! what is this? A masked man!

PROMETHEUS Can you see any god behind me?

PISTHETÆRUS No, none. But who are you, pray?

PROMETHEUS What's the time, please?

PISTHETÆRUS The time? Why, it's past noon. Who are you?

PROMETHEUS Is it the fall of day? Is it no later than that?[4]

PISTHETÆRUS Oh! 'pon my word! but you grow tiresome!

PROMETHEUS What is Zeus doing? Is he dispersing the clouds or gathering them?[5]

PISTHETÆRUS Take care, lest I lose all patience.

PROMETHEUS Come, I will raise my mask.

PISTHETÆRUS Ah! my dear Prometheus!

PROMETHEUS Stop! stop! speak lower!

PISTHETÆRUS Why, what's the matter, Prometheus?

---

[1]That is, whips—Corcyra being famous for these articles.
[2]Cleonymus is a standing butt of Aristophanes' wit, both as an informer and a notorious poltroon.
[3]In allusion to the cave of the bandit Orestes; the poet terms him a hero only because of his heroic name Orestes.
[4]Prometheus wants night to come and so reduce the risk of being seen from Olympus.
[5]The clouds would prevent Zeus seeing what was happening below him.

PROMETHEUS   H'sh, h'sh! Don't call me by my name; you will be my ruin, if Zeus should see me here. But, if you want me to tell you how things are going in heaven, take this umbrella and shield me, so that the gods don't see me.

PISTHETÆRUS   I can recognize Prometheus in this cunning trick. Come, quick then, and fear nothing; speak on.

PROMETHEUS   Then listen.

PISTHETÆRUS   I am listening, proceed!

PROMETHEUS   It's all over with Zeus.

PISTHETÆRUS   Ah! and since when, pray?

PROMETHEUS   Since you founded this city in the air. There is not a man who now sacrifices to the gods; the smoke of the victims no longer reaches us. Not the smallest offering comes! We fast as though it were the festival of Demeter.[1] The barbarian gods, who are dying of hunger, are bawling like Illyrians[2] and threaten to make an armed descent upon Zeus, if he does not open markets where joints of the victims are sold.

PISTHETÆRUS   What! there are other gods besides you, barbarian gods who dwell above Olympus?

PROMETHEUS   If there were no barbarian gods, who would be the patron of Execestides?[3]

PISTHETÆRUS   And what is the name of these gods?

PROMETHEUS   Their name? Why, the Triballi.[4]

PISTHETÆRUS   Ah, indeed! 'tis from that no doubt that we derive the word 'tribulation.'[5]

PROMETHEUS   Most likely. But one thing I can tell you for certain, namely, that Zeus and the celestial Triballi are going to send deputies here to sue for peace. Now don't you treat, unless Zeus restores the sceptre to the birds and gives you Basileia[6] in marriage.

PISTHETÆRUS   Who is this Basileia?

PROMETHEUS   A very fine young damsel, who makes the lightning for Zeus; all things come from her, wisdom, good laws, virtue, the fleet, calumnies, the public paymaster and the triobolus.

PISTHETÆRUS   Ah! then she is a sort of general manageress to the god.

PROMETHEUS   Yes, precisely. If he gives you her for your wife, yours

---

[1] The third day of the festival of Demeter was a fast.
[2] A semi-savage people, addicted to violence and brigandage.
[3] Who, being reputed a stranger despite his pretension to the title of a citizen, could only have a strange god for his patron or tutelary deity.
[4] The Triballi were a Thracian people; it was a term commonly used in Athens to describe coarse men, obscene debauchees and greedy parasites.
[5] There is a similar pun in the Greek.
[6] i.e. the *supremacy* of Greece, the real object of the war.

will be the almighty power. That is what I have come to tell you; for you know my constant and habitual goodwill towards men.

PISTHETÆRUS   Oh, yes! 'tis thanks to you that we roast our meat.[1]

PROMETHEUS   I hate the gods, as you know.

PISTHETÆRUS   Aye, by Zeus, you have always detested them.

PROMETHEUS   Towards them I am a veritable Timon;[2] but I must return in all haste, so give me the umbrella; if Zeus should see me from up there, he would think I was escorting one of the Canephori.[3]

PISTHETÆRUS   Wait, take this stool as well.

CHORUS   Near by the land of the Sciapodes[4] there is a marsh, from the borders whereof the odious Socrates evokes the souls of men. Pisander[5] came one day to see his soul, which he had left there when still alive. He offered a little victim, a camel,[6] slit his throat and, following the example of Ulysses, stepped one pace backwards.[7] Then that bat of a Chærephon[8] came up from hell to drink the camel's blood.

POSIDON[9]   This is the city of Nephelococcygia, Cloud-cuckoo-town, whither we come as ambassadors. [To TRIBALLUS.] Hi! what are you up to? you are throwing your cloak over the left shoulder. Come, fling it quick over the right! And why, pray, does it draggle in this

[1]Prometheus had stolen the fire from the gods to gratify mankind.

[2]A celebrated misanthrope, contemporary to Aristophanes. Hating the society of men, he had only a single friend, Apimantus, to whom he was attached, because of their similarity of character; he also liked Alcibiades, because he foresaw that this young man would be the ruin of his country.

[3]The Canephori were young maidens, chosen from the first families of the city, who carried baskets wreathed with myrtle at the feast of Athené, while at those of Bacchus and Demeter they appeared with gilded baskets.—The daughters of 'Metics,' or resident aliens, walked behind them, carrying an umbrella and a stool.

[4]According to Ctesias, the Sciapodes were a people who dwelt on the borders of the Atlantic. Their feet were larger than the rest of their bodies, and to shield themselves from the sun's rays they held up one of their feet as an umbrella.—By giving the Socratic philosophers the name of Sciapodes here (a name deriving from the Greek words for *feet* and *shadow*), Aristophanes wishes to convey that they are walking in the dark and busying themselves with the greatest nonsense.

[5]This Pisander was a notorious coward; for this reason the poet jestingly supposes that he had lost his soul, the seat of courage.

[6]Considering the shape and height of the camel, it can certainly not be included in the list of *small* victims, e.g. the sheep and the goat.

[7]In the evocation of the dead, Book XI of the Odyssey.

[8]Chærephon was given this same title by the Herald earlier in this comedy.—Aristophanes supposes him to have come from hell because he is lean and pallid.

[9]Posidon appears on the stage accompanied by Heracles and a Triballian god.

fashion? Have you ulcers to hide like Læspodias?[1] Oh! democracy![2] whither, oh! whither are you leading us? Is it possible that the gods have chosen such an envoy?

TRIBALLUS   Leave me alone.

POSIDON   Ugh! the cursed savage! you are by far the most barbarous of all the gods.—Tell me, Heracles, what are we going to do?

HERACLES   I have already told you that I want to strangle the fellow who has dared to block us in.

POSIDON   But, my friend, we are envoys of peace.

HERACLES   All the more reason why I wish to strangle him.

PISTHETÆRUS   Hand me the cheese-grater; bring me the silphium for sauce; pass me the cheese and watch the coals.[3]

HERACLES   Mortal! we who greet you are three gods.

PISTHETÆRUS   Wait a bit till I have prepared my silphium pickle.

HERACLES   What are these meats?[4]

PISTHETÆRUS   These are birds that have been punished with death for attacking the people's friends.

HERACLES   And you are seasoning them before answering us?

PISTHETÆRUS   Ah! Heracles! welcome, welcome! What's the matter?[5]

HERACLES   The gods have sent us here as ambassadors to treat for peace.

A SERVANT   There's no more oil in the flask.

PISTHETÆRUS   And yet the birds must be thoroughly basted with it.[6]

HERACLES   We have no interest to serve in fighting you; as for you, be friends and we promise that you shall always have rain-water in your pools and the warmest of warm weather. So far as these points go we are armed with plenary authority.

PISTHETÆRUS   We have never been the aggressors, and even now we are as well disposed for peace as yourselves, provided you agree to one equitable condition, namely, that Zeus yield his sceptre to the birds. If only this is agreed to, I invite the ambassadors to dinner.

HERACLES   That's good enough for me. I vote for peace.

POSIDON   You wretch! you are nothing but a fool and a glutton. Do you want to dethrone your own father?

PISTHETÆRUS   What an error! Why, the gods will be much more

---

[1]An Athenian general.—Neptune is trying to give Triballus some notions of elegance and good behaviour.

[2]Aristophanes supposes that democracy is in the ascendant in Olympus as it is in Athens.

[3]He is addressing his servant, Manes.

[4]Heracles softens at sight of the food.—Heracles is the glutton of the comic poets.

[5]He pretends not to have seen them at first, being so much engaged with his cookery.

[6]He pretends to forget the presence of the ambassadors.

powerful if the birds govern the earth. At present the mortals are hidden beneath the clouds, escape your observation, and commit perjury in your name; but if you had the birds for your allies, and a man, after having sworn by the crow and Zeus, should fail to keep his oath, the crow would dive down upon him unawares and pluck out his eye.

POSIDON Well thought of, by Posidon![1]

HERACLES My notion too.

PISTHETÆRUS [*to the* TRIBALLIAN] And you, what's your opinion?

TRIBALLUS Nabaisatreu.[2]

PISTHETÆRUS D'you see? he also approves. But hear another thing in which we can serve you. If a man vows to offer a sacrifice to some god, and then procrastinates, pretending that the gods can wait, and thus does not keep his word, we shall punish his stinginess.

POSIDON Ah! ah! and how?

PISTHETÆRUS While he is counting his money or is in the bath, a kite will relieve him, before he knows it, either in coin or in clothes, of the value of a couple of sheep, and carry it to the god.

HERACLES I vote for restoring them the sceptre.

POSIDON Ask the Triballian.

HERACLES Hi! Triballian, do you want a thrashing?

TRIBALLUS Saunaka baktarikrousa.

HERACLES He says, "Right willingly."

POSIDON If that be the opinion of both of you, why, I consent too.

HERACLES Very well! we accord the sceptre.

PISTHETÆRUS Ah! I was nearly forgetting another condition. I will leave Heré to Zeus, but only if the young Basileia is given me in marriage.

POSIDON Then you don't want peace. Let us withdraw.

PISTHETÆRUS It matters mighty little to me. Cook, look to the gravy.

HERACLES What an odd fellow this Posidon is! Where are you off to? Are we going to war about a woman?

POSIDON What else is there to do?

HERACLES What else? Why, conclude peace.

POSIDON Oh! the ninny! do you always want to be fooled? Why, you are seeking your own downfall. If Zeus were to die, after having yielded them the sovereignty, you would be ruined, for you are the heir of all the wealth he will leave behind.

PISTHETÆRUS Oh! by the gods! how he is cajoling you. Step aside, that I may have a word with you. Your uncle is getting the better of

---

[1]Posidon jestingly swears by himself.
[2]The barbarian god utters some gibberish which Pisthetærus interprets into consent.

you, my poor friend.[1] The law will not allow you an obolus of the paternal property, for you are a bastard and not a legitimate child.

HERACLES   I a bastard! What's that you tell me?

PISTHETÆRUS   Why, certainly; are you not born of a stranger woman? Besides, is not Athené recognized as Zeus' sole heiress? And no daughter would be that, if she had a legitimate brother.

HERACLES   But what if my father wished to give me his property on his death-bed, even though I be a bastard?

PISTHETÆRUS   The law forbids it, and this same Posidon would be the first to lay claim to his wealth, in virtue of being his legitimate brother. Listen; thus runs Solon's law: "A bastard shall not inherit, if there are legitimate children; and if there are no legitimate children, the property shall pass to the nearest kin."[2]

HERACLES   And I get nothing whatever of the paternal property?

PISTHETÆRUS   Absolutely nothing. But tell me, has your father had you entered on the registers of his phratria?[3]

HERACLES   No, and I have long been surprised at the omission.

PISTHETÆRUS   What ails you, that you should shake your fist at heaven? Do you want to fight it? Why, be on my side, I will make you a king and will feed you on bird's milk and honey.

HERACLES   Your further condition seems fair to me. I cede you the young damsel.

POSIDON   But I, I vote against this opinion.

PISTHETÆRUS   Then all depends on the Triballian. [*To the* TRIBALLIAN.] What do you say?

TRIBALLUS   Big bird give daughter pretty and queen.

HERACLES   You say that you give her?

POSIDON   Why no, he does not say anything of the sort, that he gives her; else I cannot understand any better than the swallows.

PISTHETÆRUS   Exactly so. Does he not say she must be given to the swallows?

POSIDON   Very well! you two arrange the matter; make peace, since you wish it so; I'll hold my tongue.

HERACLES   We are of a mind to grant you all that you ask. But come up there with us to receive Basileia and the celestial bounty.

PISTHETÆRUS   Here are birds already cut up, and very suitable for a nuptial feast.

---

[1] Heracles, the god of strength, was far from being remarkable in the way of cleverness.
[2] This was Athenian law.
[3] The poet attributes to the gods the same customs as those which governed Athens, and according to which no child was looked upon as legitimate unless his father had entered him on the registers of his phratria. The phratria was a division of the tribe and consisted of thirty families.

HERACLES You go and, if you like, I will stay here to roast them.

PISTHETÆRUS You to roast them! you are too much the glutton; come along with us.

HERACLES Ah! how well I would have treated myself!

PISTHETÆRUS Let some bring me a beautiful and magnificent tunic for the wedding.

CHORUS[1] At Phanæ[2], near the Clepsydra,[3] there dwells a people who have neither faith nor law, the Englottogastors,[4] who reap, sow, pluck the vines and the figs[5] with their tongues; they belong to a barbaric race, and among them the Philippi and the Gorgiases[6] are to be found; 'tis these Englottogastorian Philippi who introduced the custom all over Attica of cutting out the tongue separately at sacrifices.[7]

A MESSENGER Oh, you, whose unbounded happiness I cannot express in words, thrice happy race of airy birds, receive your king in your fortunate dwellings. More brilliant than the brightest star that illumes the earth, he is approaching his glittering golden palace; the sun itself does not shine with more dazzling glory. He is entering with his bride at his side,[8] whose beauty no human tongue can express; in his hand he brandishes the lightning, the winged shaft of Zeus; perfumes of unspeakable sweetness pervade the ethereal realms. 'Tis a glorious spectacle to see the clouds of incense wafting in light whirlwinds before the breath of the Zephyr! But here he is himself. Divine Muse! let thy sacred lips begin with songs of happy omen.

CHORUS Fall back! to the right! to the left! advance![9] Fly around this happy mortal, whom Fortune loads with her blessings. Oh! oh! what grace! what beauty! Oh, marriage so auspicious for our city! All honour to this man! 'tis through him that the birds are called to such glorious destinies. Let your nuptial hymns, your nuptial songs, greet him and his Basileia! 'Twas in the midst of such festivities that the Fates formerly united Olympian Heré to the King who governs the gods from the summit of his inaccessible throne. Oh! Hymen! oh!

---

[1]The chorus continues to tell what it has seen on its flights.

[2]The harbor of the island of Chios; but this name (from the Greek verb, *to denounce*) is used here in the sense of being the land of informers.

[3]i.e. near the orators' platform in the Public Assembly, because there stood the water-clock, by which speeches were limited.

[4]A coined name made up of the words *tongue* and *stomach*, and meaning those who fill their stomach with what they gain with their tongues, to wit, the orators.

[5]The Greek word for *fig* forms part of the Greek word for *informer*.

[6]Both rhetoricians.

[7]Because they consecrated it specially to the god of eloquence.

[8]Basileia, whom he brings back from heaven.

[9]Terms used in regulating a dance.

Hymenæus! Rosy Eros with the golden wings held the reins and guided the chariot; 'twas he, who presided over the union of Zeus and the fortunate Heré. Oh! Hymen! oh! Hymenæus!

PISTHETÆRUS   I am delighted with your songs, I applaud your verses. Now celebrate the thunder that shakes the earth, the flaming lightning of Zeus and the terrible flashing thunderbolt.

CHORUS   Oh, thou golden flash of the lightning! oh, ye divine shafts of flame, that Zeus has hitherto shot forth! Oh, ye rolling thunders, that bring down the rain! 'Tis by the order of *our* king that ye shall now stagger the earth! Oh, Hymen! 'tis through thee that he commands the universe and that he makes Basileia, whom he has robbed from Zeus, take her seat at his side. Oh! Hymen! oh! Hymenæus!

PISTHETÆRUS   Let all the winged tribes of our fellow-citizens follow the bridal couple to the palace of Zeus[1] and to the nuptial couch! Stretch forth your hands, my dear wife! Take hold of me by my wings and let us dance; I am going to lift you up and carry you through the air.

CHORUS   Oh, joy! Io Pæan! Tralala! victory is thine, oh, thou greatest of the gods!

[1]Where Pisthetærus is henceforth to reign.

DOVER·THRIFT·EDITIONS

FICTION

MADAME BOVARY, Gustave Flaubert. 256pp. 29257-6 $2.00

WHERE ANGELS FEAR TO TREAD, E. M. Forster. 128pp. (Available in U.S. only) 27791-7 $1.50

A ROOM WITH A VIEW, E. M. Forster. 176pp. (Available in U.S. only) 28467-0 $2.00

THE OVERCOAT AND OTHER STORIES, Nikolai Gogol. 112pp. 27057-2 $1.50

GREAT GHOST STORIES, John Grafton (ed.). 112pp. 27270-2 $1.00

"THE MOONLIT ROAD" AND OTHER GHOST AND HORROR STORIES, Ambrose Bierce (John Grafton, ed.) 96pp. 40056-5 $1.00

THE MABINOGION, Lady Charlotte E. Guest. 192pp. 29541-9 $2.00

WINESBURG, OHIO, Sherwood Anderson. 160pp. 28269-4 $2.00

THE LUCK OF ROARING CAMP AND OTHER STORIES, Bret Harte. 96pp. 27271-0 $1.00

THIS SIDE OF PARADISE, F. Scott Fitzgerald. 208pp. 28999-0 $2.00

"THE DIAMOND AS BIG AS THE RITZ" AND OTHER STORIES, F. Scott Fitzgerald. 29991-0 $2.00

THE SCARLET LETTER, Nathaniel Hawthorne. 192pp. 28048-9 $2.00

YOUNG GOODMAN BROWN AND OTHER STORIES, Nathaniel Hawthorne. 128pp. 27060-2 $1.00

THE GIFT OF THE MAGI AND OTHER SHORT STORIES, O. Henry. 96pp. 27061-0 $1.00

THE NUTCRACKER AND THE GOLDEN POT, E. T. A. Hoffmann. 128pp. 27806-9 $1.00

THE BEAST IN THE JUNGLE AND OTHER STORIES, Henry James. 128pp. 27552-3 $1.00

DAISY MILLER, Henry James. 64pp. 28773-4 $1.00

WASHINGTON SQUARE, Henry James. 176pp. 40431-5 $2.00

THE TURN OF THE SCREW, Henry James. 96pp. 26684-2 $1.00

DUBLINERS, James Joyce. 160pp. 26870-5 $1.00

A PORTRAIT OF THE ARTIST AS A YOUNG MAN, James Joyce. 192pp. 28050-0 $2.00

DEATH IN VENICE, Thomas Mann. 96pp. (Available in U.S. only) 28714-9 $1.00

THE METAMORPHOSIS AND OTHER STORIES, Franz Kafka. 96pp. 29030-1 $1.50

THE MAN WHO WOULD BE KING AND OTHER STORIES, Rudyard Kipling. 128pp. 28051-9 $1.50

SREDNI VASHTAR AND OTHER STORIES, Saki (H. H. Munro). 96pp. 28521-9 $1.00

THE OIL JAR AND OTHER STORIES, Luigi Pirandello. 96pp. 28459-X $1.00

SELECTED SHORT STORIES, D. H. Lawrence. 128pp. 27794-1 $1.00

GREEN TEA AND OTHER GHOST STORIES, J. Sheridan LeFanu. 96pp. 27795-X $1.00

SHORT STORIES, Theodore Dreiser. 112pp. 28215-5 $1.50

THE CALL OF THE WILD, Jack London. 64pp. 26472-6 $1.00

FIVE GREAT SHORT STORIES, Jack London. 96pp. 27063-7 $1.00

WHITE FANG, Jack London. 160pp. 26968-X $1.00

THE NECKLACE AND OTHER SHORT STORIES, Guy de Maupassant. 128pp. 27064-5 $1.00

BARTLEBY AND BENITO CERENO, Herman Melville. 112pp. 26473-4 $1.00

THE GOLD-BUG AND OTHER TALES, Edgar Allan Poe. 128pp. 26875-6 $1.00

TALES OF TERROR AND DETECTION, Edgar Allan Poe. 96pp. 28744-0 $1.00

DETECTION BY GASLIGHT, Douglas G. Greene (ed.). 272pp. 29928-7 $2.00

THE THIRTY-NINE STEPS, John Buchan. 96pp. 28201-5 $1.00

THE QUEEN OF SPADES AND OTHER STORIES, Alexander Pushkin. 128pp. 28054-3 $1.50

FIRST LOVE AND DIARY OF A SUPERFLUOUS MAN, Ivan Turgenev. 96pp. 28775-0 $1.50

FATHERS AND SONS, Ivan Turgenev. 176pp. 40073-5 $2.00

FRANKENSTEIN, Mary Shelley. 176pp. 28211-2 $1.00

THREE LIVES, Gertrude Stein. 176pp. (Available in U.S. only) 28059-4 $2.00

DOVER · THRIFT · EDITIONS

FICTION

THE STRANGE CASE OF DR. JEKYLL AND MR. HYDE, Robert Louis Stevenson. 64pp. 26688-5 $1.00

TREASURE ISLAND, Robert Louis Stevenson. 160pp. 27559-0 $1.50

THE LOST WORLD, Arthur Conan Doyle. 176pp. 40060-3 $1.50

GULLIVER'S TRAVELS, Jonathan Swift. 240pp. 29273-8 $2.00

ROBINSON CRUSOE, Daniel Defoe. 288pp. 40427-7 $2.00

THE KREUTZER SONATA AND OTHER SHORT STORIES, Leo Tolstoy. 144pp. 27805-0 $1.50

THE IMMORALIST, André Gide. 112pp. (Available in U.S. only) 29237-1 $1.50

ADVENTURES OF HUCKLEBERRY FINN, Mark Twain. 224pp. 28061-6 $2.00

THE ADVENTURES OF TOM SAWYER, Mark Twain. 192pp. 40077-8 $2.00

THE MYSTERIOUS STRANGER AND OTHER STORIES, Mark Twain. 128pp. 27069-6 $1.00

HUMOROUS STORIES AND SKETCHES, Mark Twain. 80pp. 29279-7 $1.00

YOU KNOW ME AL, Ring Lardner. 128pp. 28513-8 $1.00

MOLL FLANDERS, Daniel Defoe. 256pp. 29093-X $2.00

CANDIDE, Voltaire (François-Marie Arouet). 112pp. 26689-3 $1.00

"THE COUNTRY OF THE BLIND" AND OTHER SCIENCE-FICTION STORIES, H. G. Wells. 160pp. (Available in U.S. only) 29569-9 $1.00

THE ISLAND OF DR. MOREAU, H. G. Wells. (Available in U.S. only) 29027-1 $1.00

THE INVISIBLE MAN, H. G. Wells. 112pp. (Available in U.S. only) 27071-8 $1.00

THE TIME MACHINE, H. G. Wells. 80pp. (Available in U.S. only) 28472-7 $1.00

LOOKING BACKWARD, Edward Bellamy. 160pp. 29038-7 $2.00

THE WAR OF THE WORLDS, H. G. Wells. 160pp. (Available in U.S. only) 29506-0 $1.00

ETHAN FROME, Edith Wharton. 96pp. 26690-7 $1.00

SHORT STORIES, Edith Wharton. 128pp. 28235-X $1.00

THE AGE OF INNOCENCE, Edith Wharton. 288pp. 29803-5 $2.00

THE MOON AND SIXPENCE, W. Somerset Maugham. 176pp. (Available in U.S. only) 28731-9 $2.00

THE PICTURE OF DORIAN GRAY, Oscar Wilde. 192pp. 27807-7 $1.50

MONDAY OR TUESDAY: Eight Stories, Virginia Woolf. 64pp. (Available in U.S. only) 29453-6 $1.00

JACOB'S ROOM, Virginia Woolf. 144pp. (Available in U.S. only) 40109-X $1.50

NONFICTION

THE DEVIL'S DICTIONARY, Ambrose Bierce. 144pp. 27542-6 $1.00

DE PROFUNDIS, Oscar Wilde. 64pp. 29308-4 $1.00

OSCAR WILDE'S WIT AND WISDOM: A Book of Quotations, Oscar Wilde. 64pp. 40146-4 $1.00

THE SOULS OF BLACK FOLK, W. E. B. Du Bois. 176pp. 28041-1 $2.00

NARRATIVE OF THE LIFE OF FREDERICK DOUGLASS, Frederick Douglass. 96pp. 28499-9 $1.00

NARRATIVE OF SOJOURNER TRUTH, Sojourner Truth. 80pp. 29899-X $1.00

UP FROM SLAVERY, Booker T. Washington. 160pp. 28738-6 $2.00

A VINDICATION OF THE RIGHTS OF WOMAN, Mary Wollstonecraft. 224pp. 29036-0 $2.00

THE SUBJECTION OF WOMEN, John Stuart Mill. 112pp. 29601-6 $1.50

TAO TE CHING, Lao Tze. 112pp. 29792-6 $1.00

THE ANALECTS, Confucius. 128pp. 28484-0 $2.00

SELF-RELIANCE AND OTHER ESSAYS, Ralph Waldo Emerson. 128pp. 27790-9 $1.00

SELECTED ESSAYS, Michel de Montaigne. 96pp. 29109-X $1.50

DOVER · THRIFT · EDITIONS

NONFICTION

A MODEST PROPOSAL AND OTHER SATIRICAL WORKS, Jonathan Swift. 64pp. 28759-9 $1.00

UTOPIA, Sir Thomas More. 96pp. 29583-4 $1.50

THE AUTOBIOGRAPHY OF BENJAMIN FRANKLIN, Benjamin Franklin. 144pp. 29073-5 $1.50

COMMON SENSE, Thomas Paine. 64pp. 29602-4 $1.00

THE STORY OF MY LIFE, Helen Keller. 80pp. 29249-5 $1.00

GREAT SPEECHES, Abraham Lincoln. 112pp. 26872-1 $1.00

THE PRINCE, Niccolò Machiavelli. 80pp. 27274-5 $1.00

PRAGMATISM, William James. 128pp. 28270-8 $1.50

TOTEM AND TABOO, Sigmund Freud. 176pp. (Available in U.S. only) 40434-X $2.00

POETICS, Aristotle. 64pp. 29577-X $1.00

NICOMACHEAN ETHICS, Aristotle. 256pp. 40096-4 $2.00

MEDITATIONS, Marcus Aurelius. 128pp. 29823-X $1.50

SYMPOSIUM AND PHAEDRUS, Plato. 96pp. 27798-4 $1.50

THE TRIAL AND DEATH OF SOCRATES: Four Dialogues, Plato. 128pp. 27066-1 $1.00

THE BIRTH OF TRAGEDY, Friedrich Nietzsche. 96pp. 28515-4 $1.50

BEYOND GOOD AND EVIL: Prelude to a Philosophy of the Future, Friedrich Nietzsche. 176pp. 29868-X $1.50

CONFESSIONS OF AN ENGLISH OPIUM EATER, Thomas De Quincey. 80pp. 28742-4 $1.00

CIVIL DISOBEDIENCE AND OTHER ESSAYS, Henry David Thoreau. 96pp. 27563-9 $1.00

SELECTIONS FROM THE JOURNALS (Edited by Walter Harding), Herny David Thoreau. 96pp. 28760-2 $1.00

WALDEN; OR, LIFE IN THE WOODS, Henry David Thoreau. 224pp. 28495-6 $2.00

THE LAND OF LITTLE RAIN, Mary Austin. 96pp. 29037-9 $1.50

THE THEORY OF THE LEISURE CLASS, Thorstein Veblen. 256pp. 28062-4 $2.00

PLAYS

PROMETHEUS BOUND, Aeschylus. 64pp. 28762-9 $1.00

THE ORESTEIA TRILOGY: Agamemnon, The Libation-Bearers and The Furies, Aeschylus. 160pp. 29242-8 $1.50

LYSISTRATA, Aristophanes. 64pp. 28225-2 $1.00

WHAT EVERY WOMAN KNOWS, James Barrie. 80pp. (Available in U.S. only) 29578-8 $1.50

THE CHERRY ORCHARD, Anton Chekhov. 64pp. 26682-6 $1.00

THE THREE SISTERS, Anton Chekhov. 64pp. 27544-2 $1.00

UNCLE VANYA, Anton Chekhov. 64pp. 40159-6 $1.50

THE INSPECTOR GENERAL, Nikolai Gogol. 80pp. 28500-6 $1.50

THE WAY OF THE WORLD, William Congreve. 80pp. 27787-9 $1.50

BACCHAE, Euripides. 64pp. 29580-X $1.00

MEDEA, Euripides. 64pp. 27548-5 $1.00

THE MIKADO, William Schwenck Gilbert. 64pp. 27268-0 $1.50

FAUST, PART ONE, Johann Wolfgang von Goethe. 192pp. 28046-2 $2.00

SHE STOOPS TO CONQUER, Oliver Goldsmith. 80pp. 26867-5 $1.50

A DOLL'S HOUSE, Henrik Ibsen. 80pp. 27062-9 $1.00

HEDDA GABLER, Henrik Ibsen. 80pp. 26469-6 $1.50

GHOSTS, Henrik Ibsen. 64pp. 29852-3 $1.50

VOLPONE, Ben Jonson. 112pp. 28049-7 $1.50

DR. FAUSTUS, Christopher Marlowe. 64pp. 28208-2 $1.00

THE MISANTHROPE, Molière. 64pp. 27065-3 $1.00

DOVER·THRIFT·EDITIONS

PLAYS

THE EMPEROR JONES, Eugene O'Neill. 64pp. 29268-1 $1.50

BEYOND THE HORIZON, Eugene O'Neill. 96pp. 29085-9 $1.50

ANNA CHRISTIE, Eugene O'Neill. 80pp. 29985-6 $1.50

THE LONG VOYAGE HOME AND OTHER PLAYS, Eugene O'Neill. 80pp. 28755-6 $1.00

RIGHT YOU ARE, IF YOU THINK YOU ARE, Luigi Pirandello. 64pp. (Available in U.S. only) 29576-1 $1.50

SIX CHARACTERS IN SEARCH OF AN AUTHOR, Luigi Pirandello. 64pp. (Available in U.S. only) 29992-9 $1.50

HANDS AROUND, Arthur Schnitzler. 64pp. 28724-6 $1.00

ANTONY AND CLEOPATRA, William Shakespeare. 128pp. 40062-X $1.50

HAMLET, William Shakespeare. 128pp. 27278-8 $1.00

HENRY IV, William Shakespeare. 96pp. 29584-2 $1.00

RICHARD III, William Shakespeare. 112pp. 28747-5 $1.00

OTHELLO, William Shakespeare. 112pp. 29097-2 $1.00

JULIUS CAESAR, William Shakespeare. 80pp. 26876-4 $1.00

KING LEAR, William Shakespeare. 112pp. 28058-6 $1.00

MACBETH, William Shakespeare. 96pp. 27802-6 $1.00

THE MERCHANT OF VENICE, William Shakespeare. 96pp. 28492-1 $1.00

A MIDSUMMER NIGHT'S DREAM, William Shakespeare. 80pp. 27067-X $1.00

MUCH ADO ABOUT NOTHING, William Shakespeare. 80pp. 28272-4 $1.00

AS YOU LIKE IT, William Shakespeare. 80pp. 40432-3 $1.50

THE TAMING OF THE SHREW, William Shakespeare. 96pp. 29765-9 $1.00

TWELFTH NIGHT; OR, WHAT YOU WILL, William Shakespeare. 80pp. 29290-8 $1.00

ROMEO AND JULIET, William Shakespeare. 96pp. 27557-4 $1.00

ARMS AND THE MAN, George Bernard Shaw. 80pp. (Available in U.S. only) 26476-9 $1.50

PYGMALION, George Bernard Shaw. 96pp. (Available in U.S. only) 28222-8 $1.00

HEARTBREAK HOUSE, George Bernard Shaw. 128pp. (Available in U.S. only) 29291-6 $1.50

THE SCHOOL FOR SCANDAL, Richard Brinsley Sheridan. 96pp. 26687-7 $1.50

ANTIGONE, Sophocles. 64pp. 27804-2 $1.00

OEDIPUS REX, Sophocles. 64pp. 26877-2 $1.00

ELECTRA, Sophocles. 64pp. 28482-4 $1.00

MISS JULIE, August Strindberg. 64pp. 27281-8 $1.50

THE PLAYBOY OF THE WESTERN WORLD AND RIDERS TO THE SEA, J. M. Synge. 80pp. 27562-0 $1.50

THE IMPORTANCE OF BEING EARNEST, Oscar Wilde. 64pp. 26478-5 $1.00

LADY WINDERMERE'S FAN, Oscar Wilde. 64pp. 40078-6 $1.00

BOXED SETS

FIVE GREAT POETS: Poems by Shakespeare, Keats, Poe, Dickinson and Whitman, Dover. 416pp. 26942-6 $5.00

NINE GREAT ENGLISH POETS: Poems by Shakespeare, Keats, Blake, Coleridge, Wordsworth, Mrs. Browning, FitzGerald, Tennyson and Kipling, Dover. 704pp. 27633-3 $9.00

FIVE GREAT ENGLISH ROMANTIC POETS, Dover. 496pp. 27893-X $5.00

SEVEN GREAT ENGLISH VICTORIAN POETS: Seven Volumes, Dover. 592pp. 40204-5 $7.50

SIX GREAT AMERICAN POETS: Poems by Poe, Dickinson, Whitman, Longfellow, Frost and Millay, Dover. 512pp. (Available in U.S. only) 27425-X $6.00